WORLD-READINESS STANDARDS FOR LEARNING LANGUAGES

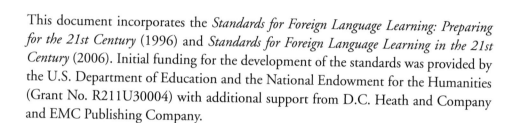

This document incorporates the *Standards for Foreign Language Learning: Preparing for the 21st Century* (1996) and *Standards for Foreign Language Learning in the 21st Century* (2006). Initial funding for the development of the standards was provided by the U.S. Department of Education and the National Endowment for the Humanities (Grant No. R211U30004) with additional support from D.C. Heath and Company and EMC Publishing Company.

The National Standards in Foreign Language Education Project is a collaborative effort of the American Association of Teachers of Arabic (AATA), American Association of Teachers of French (AATF), American Association of Teachers of German (AATG), American Association of Teachers of Italian (AATI), American Association of Teachers of Japanese (AATJ, formerly the National Council of Japanese Teachers and the Association of Teachers of Japanese), American Association of Teachers of Korean (AATK), American Association of Teachers of Modern Greek (AATMG), American Association of Teachers of Spanish and Portuguese (AATSP), American Classical League (ACL), American Council of Teachers of Russian (ACTR), American Council on the Teaching of Foreign Languages (ACTFL), American Sign Language Teachers Association (ASLTA), Chinese Language Association of Secondary-Elementary Schools (CLASS), Chinese Language Teachers Association (CLTA), Modern Language Association (MLA), National Council of Less Commonly Taught Languages (NCOLCTL), and National Standards Task Force for Hindi.

© 2015 COPYRIGHT
National Standards in Foreign Language Education Project (NSFLEP)

ISBN: 978-0-9896532-9-9
Mobi ISBN: 978-1-942544-03-6
ePub Universal ISBN: 978-1-942544-04-3
ePub iPad ISBN: 978-1-942544-05-0

Printed by the American Council on the Teaching of Foreign Languages (ACTFL), Alexandria, VA.

World-Readiness Standards for Learning Languages

TABLE OF CONTENTS

ACKNOWLEDGMENTS

Many organizations and individuals deserve recognition for their intellectual and financial support of the collaborative effort that has resulted in the production of the World-Readiness Standards for Learning Languages. We wish to thank:

- Dr. June K. Phillips for serving as the original Project Director who guided the process for creating professional collaboration and consensus resulting in the National Standards; for creating the initial draft of this updated fourth edition; and for providing her experience, insights, expertise, and perspectives that had an incredible impact on shaping the final document;

- the U.S. Department of Education and the National Endowment for the Humanities for committing the original funds that provided us with the opportunity to develop standards for the study of the world's languages, which enable American youth to take their place among multilingual societies;

- the collaborating organizations for continuing to demonstrate the power that professional unity can achieve;

- Christine Brown, chair of the original Student Standards Task Force, for leading the Standards-writing process and the original Task Force members, Advisory Council, project staff, and consultants who spent countless hours discussing, evaluating, revising, and finalizing the National Standards and creating the Standards publications;

- the numerous organizations which have endorsed the National Standards and provided input during the process of refreshing the language of the Standards;

- the national organizations that continue to create, review, and update language-specific standards to guide implementation in programs for all languages at all levels; and

- the numerous individuals who intensively examined drafts and communicated their reactions so that the resulting document reflects an overwhelming consensus of the profession.

We wish to thank all the national, state, and local organizations for supporting the National Standards in Foreign Language Education Project and using these National Standards for designing programs and learning so that all learners acquire the languages and access to cultures they need to be ready for future education, careers, and experiences around the world.

The Standards Collaborative Board

STATEMENT OF PHILOSOPHY

The following statement was developed by the original K–12 Student Standards Task Force as it began work on developing national standards for language learning. From this philosophy, the goals for language learning were derived, and all the work in standards setting relates to these concepts.

Language and communication are at the heart of the human experience. The United States must educate students who are equipped linguistically and culturally to communicate successfully in a pluralistic American society and abroad. This imperative envisions a future in which ALL students will develop and maintain proficiency in English and at least one other language, modern or classical. Learners who come from non-English-speaking backgrounds should also have opportunities to develop further proficiencies in their first language.

Supporting this vision are three assumptions about language and culture, learners of language and culture, and language and culture education:

Competence in more than one language and culture enables people to
- communicate with other people in other cultures in a variety of settings,
- look beyond their customary borders,
- develop insight into their own language and culture,
- act with greater awareness of self, of other cultures, and their own relationship to those cultures,
- gain direct access to additional bodies of knowledge, and
- participate more fully in the global community and marketplace.

All students can be successful language and culture learners, and they
- must have access to language and culture study that is integrated into the entire education experience,
- benefit from the development and maintenance of proficiency in more than one language,
- learn in a variety of ways and settings, and
- acquire proficiency at varied rates.

Language and culture education is part of the core curriculum, and it
- is tied to program models that incorporate effective strategies, assessment procedures, and technologies,
- reflects evolving standards at the national, state, and local levels, and
- develops and enhances basic communication skills and higher order thinking skills.

WORLD-READINESS STANDARDS FOR LEARNING LANGUAGES

GOAL AREAS	STANDARDS		
COMMUNICATION Communicate effectively in more than one language in order to function in a variety of situations and for multiple purposes	**Interpersonal Communication:** Learners interact and negotiate meaning in spoken, signed, or written conversations to share information, reactions, feelings, and opinions.	**Interpretive Communication:** Learners understand, interpret, and analyze what is heard, read, or viewed on a variety of topics.	**Presentational Communication:** Learners present information, concepts, and ideas to inform, explain, persuade, and narrate on a variety of topics using appropriate media and adapting to various audiences of listeners, readers, or viewers.
CULTURES Interact with cultural competence and understanding	**Relating Cultural Practices to Perspectives:** Learners use the language to investigate, explain, and reflect on the relationship between the practices and perspectives of the cultures studied.	**Relating Cultural Products to Perspectives:** Learners use the language to investigate, explain, and reflect on the relationship between the products and perspectives of the cultures studied.	
CONNECTIONS Connect with other disciplines and acquire information and diverse perspectives in order to use the language to function in academic and career-related situations	**Making Connections:** Learners build, reinforce, and expand their knowledge of other disciplines while using the language to develop critical thinking and to solve problems creatively.	**Acquiring Information and Diverse Perspectives:** Learners access and evaluate information and diverse perspectives that are available through the language and its cultures.	
COMPARISONS Develop insight into the nature of language and culture in order to interact with cultural competence	**Language Comparisons:** Learners use the language to investigate, explain, and reflect on the nature of language through comparisons of the language studied and their own.	**Cultural Comparisons:** Learners use the language to investigate, explain, and reflect on the concept of culture through comparisons of the cultures studied and their own.	
COMMUNITIES Communicate and interact with cultural competence in order to participate in multilingual communities at home and around the world	**School and Global Communities:** Learners use the language both within and beyond the classroom to interact and collaborate in their community and the globalized world.	**Lifelong Learning:** Learners set goals and reflect on their progress in using languages for enjoyment, enrichment, and advancement.	

WORLD LANGUAGES AND THE EDUCATED CITIZEN

The World-Readiness Standards for Learning Languages define the central role of world languages in the learning career of every student. The five goal areas of the Standards establish an inextricable link between communication and culture, which is applied in making connections and comparisons and in using this competence to be part of local and global communities.

> The ability to communicate with respect and cultural understanding in more than one language is an essential element of global competence. This competence is developed and demonstrated by investigating the world, recognizing and weighing perspectives, acquiring and applying disciplinary and interdisciplinary knowledge, communicating ideas, and taking action. Global competence is fundamental to the experience of learning languages whether in classrooms, through virtual connections, or via everyday experiences. Language learning contributes an important means to communicate and interact in order to participate in multilingual communities at home and around the world. This interaction develops the disposition to explore the perspectives behind the products and practices of a culture and to value such intercultural experiences. (ACTFL, 2014)

The World-Readiness Standards for Learning Languages create a roadmap to guide learners to develop competence to communicate effectively and interact with cultural competence to participate in multilingual communities at home and around the world.

The World-Readiness Standards for Learning Languages provide the framework for a curriculum with the richness and depth to provide a broad range of communicative experiences and content knowledge. These Standards put the focus on the broader view of second language study and competence: What should learners know and be able to do—and how well? The Standards provide a purpose for learning another language, establishing a broader, more complete rationale for language education to guide parents, educators, administrators, and community members to develop and support language learners through the design of effective programs and options to learn, practice, and apply this competence.

How is this competence critical for today's citizens? The businessperson, the poet, the emergency room nurse, the diplomat, the scientist, and the teenage user of social media are representative Americans who play diverse roles in life, yet each could present a convincing rationale for the importance of learning languages beyond their own.

Their reasons might range from the practical to the idealistic, but one simple truth gives substance to them all: To relate in a meaningful way to another human being, one must be able to communicate effectively and interact with cultural competence and understanding.

From the flowing green lawns and porch swings of rural America to the front stoops of cities, ours has traditionally been a culture of openness, of passing the time of day with friends who stroll by. But today the whole world strolls by, not just physically but through social media that connect individuals from around the world in real or delayed time. People may come to our doors to question and discuss, to request our aid, but more likely they tweet or text to get our attention. Digital and direct communication lead in both directions; we are going out into the wide world to run our errands. The neighborhood language of the front porch will no longer serve to transact world business or to make new friends. We must acquire the ability to understand and to be understood in the languages of the worldwide neighborhood.

To study another language and culture gives one the powerful key to successful communication: *knowing how, when, and why, to say what to whom.* All the linguistic and social knowledge required for effective human-to-human interaction is encompassed in those 10 words. Formerly, most teaching in language classrooms concentrated on the *how* (grammar) to say *what* (vocabulary). While these components of language remain crucial, the current organizing principle for language study is communication, which also highlights the *why* (purpose), the to *whom* (audience), and the *when* (context), encompassing the sociolinguistic and cultural aspects of language. The Standards' approach to world language instruction is designed to facilitate genuine interaction with others, whether they are on another continent, across town, or within the neighborhood, and whether they are face-to-face, connected electronically, or availing themselves of another's written or broadcast messages.

To study another language and culture enhances one's personal education in many ways. By learning a new linguistic system, an individual acquires an objective view of his or her native language. For someone who has never learned another language, this point is difficult to comprehend; for those who have learned a new language, it is manifestly clear. The structural bones of one's language, the limits to the range of ideas expressible in that language, the intense interdependence of language and culture—all of these concepts become apparent as one acquires another language. The learner becomes aware of the ways in which language speakers adroitly switch levels of discourse as the context of communication changes. The contributions of volume, pitch, speed, and tone of voice to the emotional layers of language become clear. The language learner also realizes that eye contact, facial expressions, and gestures play a vital role in enhancing the message that is being conveyed. With these understandings comes a new-found respect for the beauty and grace of others' languages, as well as one's own.

The study of classical languages (Latin and Ancient Greek) maintains a viable position in language programs from elementary schools through postsecondary institutions. While the main conduit through which learners communicate with the ancient world is through reading their literature, many educators have their learners practice the language through activities involving speaking and writing. The insights into language development, the interaction with ancient civilizations through their literature and history, and the cross-cultural understanding that results from the study of these languages are all compelling reasons for the inclusion of classical language instruction in the curricula at any level.

Research indicates that the very process of studying another language may give learners a cognitive boost that enables them to perform at higher levels in some other subjects. One study (Cooper, Yanosky, Wisenbaker, Jahner, Webb, & Wilbur, 2008) investigated the relationship of world language learning and verbal ability as measured on the verbal portion of the Scholastic Aptitude Test (SAT). They looked at Preliminary-SAT (PSAT) scores of students as well and found that students who studied a language scored higher than those who did not. Additionally, students with lower PSAT scores benefited most from studying a language—a finding which reinforces that language study should be open to all students and not just those who excel in English language skills. Additional studies show that over time second language learners (1) have improved test scores; (2) are able to think divergently; and (3) achieve in their first language (Cade, 1997). Curtain and Dahlberg (2010), report on a number of studies that show correlations between foreign language study and other academic areas as measured on standardized tests, especially with English language arts and mathematics. Most of these studies were done with elementary school children and held firm regardless of race, gender, or socio-economic background. The data are correlational so they do not prove causality but do support that achievement coalesces around a curriculum that includes world language study.

More extensive research that investigates how learners pursue a variety of tasks, and is not limited to test scores, has been done with bilingual children. Bialystok with colleagues and graduate students in Canada has been investigating ways in which bilinguals and monolinguals carry out tasks. She concludes that bilinguals are more advanced in solving problems requiring the inhibition of misleading information (Bialystok, 2005) and in solving experimental problems requiring high levels of control (Bialystok, 1999). More recently, she has expanded her research from a focus on bilinguals to students in immersion programs where the kinds of metalinguistic advantages held by bilinguals could be seen to emerge among immersion learners (Bialystok, Peets, & Moreno, 2012). The immersion students with only three years in the program also did better than monolinguals on a number of tasks related to executive control. This research becomes more relevant to world language programs since most students are not bilingual so results cannot be generalized. However, the immersion model holds promise.

In the future, researchers will be able to go beyond academic, test-based correlational studies and the cognitive task-based investigations into studies that can actually see how the brain is processing in individuals who are learning and using second languages. In Sweden, MRI scans taken before and after three months of intensive language study by military students showed that parts of the brain grew (Mårtensson, Eriksson, Bodammer, Lindgren, Johansson, Nyberg, & Lövdén, 2012). Again this is a specialized group of students under intensive learning conditions but suggests new ways of investigating language learning and thinking.

To study another language and culture provides access to a wide variety of authentic literary and informational texts, as well as film and video as they are experienced by the audience for whom they were created. Irony, humor, satire, and other rich textures of prose are revealed at their deepest level only to those familiar with both the language and culture. Similarly, the subtle seasonings that flavor drama, song, and poetry are discernible only to those who know the language of the playwright, lyricist, and the poet. To study another language and culture increases enormously one's ability to see these aspects beyond the literal meaning of the words. When learners access and use these culturally authentic sources, they are building their literacy skills at the same time.

Since the content of a language course potentially deals with history, geography, social studies, science, mathematics, and the visual and performing arts, it is easy for learners to develop an interdisciplinary perspective at the same time they are gaining intercultural understandings. Pedagogically, this content is enhanced by the methods used to teach languages today in any learning environment: the use of images and items from real life for sharpening perception, a wide variety of physical activities and games, involvement in role play and other dramatic activities, the use of music in both receptive and participatory modes of communication, and learning experiences that call for collaboration, creativity, critical thinking and problem solving as well as both inductive and deductive reasoning. This broad range of language learning strategies appeals to a variety of learning styles and expands the learners' awareness of the many dimensions of their own intelligence.

To study another language and culture is to gain an especially rich preparation for the future. It is difficult to imagine a job, a profession, a career, or a leisure activity which will not be enhanced greatly by the ability to communicate efficiently and sensitively with others. While it is impossible for students to foresee which languages will be useful at a later point in life, those who have once experienced the process of acquiring a second language have gained language learning skills that make learning additional languages easier. Knowing how to learn a language, suspending the need to know every word, constantly seeking to collect clues to put together a comprehensive picture of meaning, using what one knows about the language to express new ideas in creative ways using limited language—these are the skills that serve a language learner in future situations where the language or culture is not known very well. Possessing the linguistic and cultural insights that come with the study of one or more world languages will be a requisite for life as an informed, productive, and globally literate citizen in the worldwide community.

THE DEVELOPMENT OF STANDARDS

In 1993, foreign language education became the seventh and final subject area to receive federal funding to develop National Standards for students in kindergarten through 12th grade. An 11-member task force, representing a variety of languages, levels of instruction, program models, and geographic regions, was appointed to undertake the enormous task of defining **content standards**—what students should know and be able to do—in foreign language education in Grades 4, 8, and 12. These Standards were intended to serve as a gauge for excellence, as states and local districts carried out their responsibilities for curriculum in the schools. The original 1996 publication accomplished under the federal grant was published as a "generic" set of standards that applied to all languages.

The Process

The members of the task force approached the development of the Standards by examining first the skills and knowledge that language education should prepare students with in the 21st century where global competencies are at the fore: They identified the broad goals of the discipline. Within each of these areas, they then identified the essential skills and knowledge students would need to acquire by the time they left the 12th grade. It is these essential skills and knowledge which comprise the Standards. At each stage of development, the task force shared its work with the profession at large. Several drafts were widely disseminated. Task force members gave literally hundreds of presentations and read through many more written comments. All comments were seriously considered, and the final document reflected many of the recommended changes.

The development of the Standards has galvanized the field of language education. The degree of involvement, and of consensus, among educators at all levels has been unprecedented. In some respects, language education was better prepared than other disciplines to undertake standards development. Several decades of work on defining competency-based teaching and assessment has focused language educators on preparing learners who can use the language in meaningful ways and in real life situations that they will encounter in their future learning and careers. Furthermore, that work generated a dynamic discussion on the compelling rationale for language education for all learners.

Even as the National Standards were being published in 1996, the impact was being felt at the state level and within local school districts. States began almost immediately to construct standards for their public schools and, by 2011, 42 states had state world language standards strongly aligned with the National Standards (Phillips & Abbott, 2011). In turn, local districts have reconstructed curriculum, instruction, and student assessment to align with their state standards, and an increasing number of higher education programs are using the Standards in their curricular work. Additionally, growth in language programs at the elementary and middle school level can be directly tied to the earlier starts and articulated program sequencing advocated in the state and National Standards. In essence, the National Standards have become the common set of goals for the world language profession, now deeply embedded in school curriculum, university syllabi, as well as teacher certification.

New Editions of Standards

Subsequent to the publication in 1996 of *Standards for Foreign Language Learning: Preparing for the 21st Century*, the collaboration of the four professional organizations that had sponsored the Standards project (American Council on the Teaching of Foreign Languages, American Association of Teachers of French, American Association of Teachers of German, American Association of Teachers of Spanish and Portuguese) was expanded to include seven others: American Association of Teachers of Italian, American Classical League, American Council of Teachers of Russian, Chinese Language Association of Secondary-Elementary Schools/ Chinese Language Teachers Association, National Council of Secondary Teachers of Japanese/ Association of Teachers of Japanese (now merged as American Association of Teachers of Japanese). These groups pursued the next steps in developing Standards by creating language-specific standards that built upon the original ones, commonly referred to as the "generic" standards. The 1999 edition of Standards, newly titled *Standards for Foreign Language Learning in the 21st Century*, included the work of these professional organizations. The 2006 edition added Standards for Arabic. Since then, other organizations have completed language-specific standards based on the common "generic" standards: the American Sign Language Teachers Association for American Sign Language; a task force on Learning Scandinavian Languages for Danish, Norwegian, and Swedish; the Korean National Standards Task Force and the American Association of Teachers of Korean for Korean; and the National Standards Task Force for Hindi. Other groups have already begun their development of standards that will assist with the implementation of programs to learn additional languages.

This current publication is an updated revision of the National Standards and is available to purchase with one set of language-specific standards or with the complete and expanding set of all language-specific standards. Readers are clearly interested in studying the standards for the specific language they teach, but are encouraged to read across languages where they will find great ideas that they can adapt. A 2011 survey to assess the impact of the National Standards on institutions, on the professional development of teachers, on classroom practice, and on the preparation of future teachers provides evidence that the change we were seeking through the Standards is occurring (Phillips & Abbott, 2011). The survey also indicated areas where the Standards could be more clearly explained and where examples could be more strongly illustrated. This print volume contains revised text to respond to observations and input from educators who provided information on that survey undertaken by ACTFL to assess the impact of the Standards. (The narrative report and the survey results are both available on the ACTFL website at *www.actfl.org*.)

WHAT'S NEW IN THIS FOURTH EDITION? WHY WORLD-READINESS?

The phrase "World-Readiness" signals that the Standards have been revised with important changes to focus on real-world applications. Learners who add another language and culture to their preparation are not only college- and career-ready, but are also "world-ready"—that is, they bring additional knowledge, skills, and dispositions to add to their resumé for entering postsecondary study or a career.

The term "World-Readiness Standards" also signals that the languages being learned are no longer "foreign"—they are the languages of many of our learners and many of our local communities. Often the languages taught within our schools are not "foreign" to many of our students (e.g., Italian, Chinese, or Spanish), nor are they "foreign" to the United States (e.g., Native American languages, American Sign Language, Spanish, or French). Increasingly, states have recognized this situation by referring to these languages as World Languages, Modern and Classical Languages, Languages Other Than English (LOTEs), or Second Languages. The terms "world language," "second language," "target language," and sometimes simply "language" are all used interchangeably to refer to languages other than English taught in U.S. institutions. Rather than focusing on what is different and unfamiliar, the goal of these Standards is to make learners confident in situations where they interact and communicate with or within other cultures.

Among the key changes or additions in this fourth edition of the Standards are the following:

1. The Standards have explicitly added attention to the development of literacy and the 21st century skills of communication, collaboration, critical thinking, and creativity.

2. The progression for developing learners' performance in the modes of communication is described through the Sample Performance Indicators

3. Sample Progress Indicators are now identified by performance range (Novice, Intermediate, and Advanced ranges) to be adaptable to any beginning point and any program model or grade configuration. The Sample Progress Indicators are further delineated through sample indicators appropriate for learners in each range in elementary grades, middle school and high school, or postsecondary levels.

Standards define the agenda for teaching and learning for the next decade—and beyond. Change will continue to be incremental, but it will accelerate if we succeed in addressing three fundamental issues that set the stage for the future: (1) the expansion of student opportunities for language learning that can occur anytime and anywhere; (2) the preparation of new teachers of all languages and at all levels within our schools; and (3) the support of practicing educators through ongoing, job-embedded professional development. The message of the Standards must permeate all of these learning experiences.

LANGUAGE LEARNING IN THE UNITED STATES

Three important issues influence language learning options and program models today:

1. Technology: The existence of language learning available on the learner's schedule, anytime and any place;
2. Longer sequences: The need for longer sequences of study to reach proficiency levels appropriate for personal growth and careers;
3. Opportunities: The number and variety of language learning opportunities available to learners.

Today's language programs need to respond to all three issues in order to ensure that learners are able to achieve the goals of the Standards.

Technology: With the ongoing expansion of both online learning opportunities and learning environments that occur anytime and anywhere, language study takes on many forms in addition to traditional classroom instruction. Language learning is available online, both in structured courses and through computer applications that individuals use for a variety of purposes, whether learning a few expressions for travel, gaming to learn additional vocabulary, or translating highly technical words and expressions to collaborate on a project. Educators are using technology to "flip the classroom" where much of the learning of new concepts occurs outside the classroom through explanations, readings, and practice activities available to the learners online. Class time is then used more for applying the new concepts through guided and individual practice.

Longer Sequences: It takes time for individual learners to develop strong second language competencies. The present patchwork quilt of language curricula in the United States comes in all shapes, sizes, and textures, with the greatest variability in both the age at which language learning may begin and the amount of time provided, defined by frequency (sessions per week) and intensity (number of minutes per day). Far too many learners have access to the study of another language beginning only at the high school level, and the majority of adolescents enroll for no more than a 2-year sequence. That pattern is shifting in many places as districts have provided earlier starting points for language learning, in elementary grades or middle schools. In some states, language learning requirements for college admission or for honors diplomas have increased. Students who start earlier have a distinct advantage because time is a critical component for developing language performance.

Opportunities: Students themselves recognize the value of another language and increasingly choose to progress beyond minimal language requirements through opportunities available both online and in a traditional classroom setting. In high schools, enrollments in elective, International Baccalaureate (IB), and Advanced Placement (AP) courses are rising. State by state, the language program options vary greatly. A survey by the Center for Applied Linguistics indicated that the number of schools offering K–8 programs decreased 1997–2008 (Rhodes & Pufahl, 2010). In contrast, school structures such as magnet schools and charter schools often incorporate language learning to various degrees as part of their focus. Programs of language immersion are increasingly available to learners at all grade levels. So, too are an increasing variety of languages, adding to the more commonly taught languages. In addition to French, German, Latin, and Spanish, students increasingly have access to learn American Sign Language, Arabic, Chinese, Hebrew, Hindi, Italian, Japanese, Korean, Modern Greek, Portuguese, and Russian. Students choose to learn any language for purposes that include connections to ethnic or regional backgrounds or communities, career plans, personal curiosity, or global importance. In increasing numbers, states are implementing a Seal of Biliteracy through which students document attainment of a specific level of language performance in both English and another language, often the students' native or heritage language. The Seal of Biliteracy provides another opportunity for recognizing and valuing language learning as an essential competence for educated citizens.

PROMISING PROGRAM MODELS FROM K–16

Opportunities to Learn K–8

Elementary school and middle school programs come in many models. The greatest variability is in the frequency (number of sessions per week) and intensity (number of minutes per session) of the experience for the learner.

Immersion Programs: Immersion programs are the most intensive, in that all or part of the curricular content is learned in the target language. Students spend 50–100% of the school day learning subject matter in the target language, which becomes acquired as it is used for learning, exploring, presenting, and discussing subject matter content. Language arts instruction adds to learners' control of the target language. Often, full immersion programs add instruction in English language arts by third grade to ensure the development of language skills in both languages. In dual language immersion programs, learners usually spend half of each day in English and half in the target language. Another variety of this model, two-way immersion, can be implemented when a sufficient number of native speakers of a language other than English are enrolled in the school; in this model, native speakers of the target language and English speakers join together to pursue classroom content in both languages.

Content-Related Programs: Content-related or content-connected language programs are less intensive than immersion models, but, like immersion programs, use subject matter content as the focus for learning and practicing the target language. So rather than teaching language in isolation (numbers, colors, school), the language comes from the connection with the grade level curriculum in science (life cycle of the butterfly), social studies (differences in communities), health (making healthy choices from food groups), or other subject areas. Like immersion programs, content-related programs use integrated thematic instruction that reinforces the elementary or middle school curriculum. These articulated programs specifically teach the target language for designated periods of time each week.

Some young people may desire to try a new language at the middle school level because they have developed an interest in a part of the world where it is spoken. The middle school should provide for entry into languages that may not have been available earlier. Adolescents who begin a third language have a distinct advantage over those beginning a second. Ideally, they now understand words as symbols that represent concepts rather than assuming that words are concepts. As students work toward the Comparisons goal in a second language, they develop insights into how languages operate and these understandings make them quite different learners of a third or fourth language. A broadening of opportunities with middle school and high school programs capitalizes on the general linguistic advantage that comes from extended study and early opportunities.

Programs in Grades 9–12

In high schools, many program models exist with new models emerging as districts implement instruction in the early grades. High schools are designing promising models to support students who want to learn a third or fourth language.

Some of the models for extended learning in high schools include:
- Advanced Placement (AP) courses that offer the possibility of college credit dependent upon national examination scores and individual college policies;
- International Baccalaureate (IB) courses that provide international content that prepares students for an international diploma based upon examination, future international study, or college credit;
- concurrent enrollments or language classes conducted in high schools by high school faculty endorsed by a local college or university which grants college credit or that allows high school students to take dual credit courses at that local college or university;
- content-based advanced courses in a world language that focus on subject matter from another discipline while continuing skill development in the language, such as exploring the culture through its media and arts or understanding the culture through current events;
- school-within-a-school models that have a world language as part of a magnet or specific program; and
- academic or magnet schools that focus on language development through a particular discipline (e.g., international marketing or health professions).

In addition, high school students often develop language and culture proficiency in other settings:
- schools for home-schooled learners that bring these students to a site where they can learn a world language that is added to content that parents can teach;
- Saturday school programs that offer language in intensive all-day or half-day sessions;
- international schools that enroll children from the United States and other nations as represented in a community;
- topic-oriented courses (e.g., conversation, business) that are not part of the regular high school sequence;

- summer camps, week-long/weekend immersion camps; and
- exchange programs and study abroad programs during the academic year or in summer.

Programs at the Postsecondary Level

Following the development of longer sequences and more opportunities to learn more languages in grades K–12, learners entering colleges and universities will have greater competencies in second languages and cultures than ever before; they also will expect to continue studies in those languages, cultures, literatures, and in other disciplines that draw upon those abilities. Colleges and universities have an exciting challenge to redesign programs in new and innovative ways. Postsecondary students want to use world languages in fields ranging from history, philosophy, business, art history, and journalism to nursing, engineering, and the sciences. Community colleges play a critical role both providing ongoing instruction in the language(s) a learner has already started and opening new opportunities for learners to start new languages. The emphasis in the World-Readiness Standards on levels of performance rather than content specific to grade levels provides guidance to lead to a seamless continuity, student-centered articulation, and higher levels of performance for poststecondary learners.

Implementing the Standards at the postsecondary level presents a unique opportunity for faculty to develop new program options.

- Some students will wish to begin the study of a new language at the postsecondary level, so institutions still need to offer basic language instruction. Many colleges and universities are doing this through affiliated centers that focus on beginning instruction in a variety of languages.
- Students who have achieved a certain degree of proficiency through an extended sequence of study need courses and programs that connect with career goals and cross-cultural ventures. Many institutions are expanding their language and literature programs into "language studies" that include content courses outside the language department with a focus on interdisciplinary work in politics, history, or economics.
- Bridge courses, often given in fifth or sixth semesters, may be appropriate for lower division students who wish to refine their language through subject-related content such as film studies, a historical period, or music history; these courses are taught by language faculty.
- Content courses are full-fledged courses given in the target language, with the greater emphasis on learning the content itself. These may be taught by language or content area specialists.
- Dual degree programs combine the traditional liberal arts education with a professional field in preparation for working in a global economy. Dual degree programs often combine study or internships abroad so that students gain the cultural, linguistic, and pragmatic job experiences that enable them to become effective citizens of the world.

All of these models and others have been set out by the Modern Language Association in an important document, *Foreign Languages and Higher Education: New Structures for a Changed World* (2007).

MULTIPLE ENTRY POINTS AND AN EXTENDED SEQUENCE OF STUDY

Sequential study for an extended period of time is the ideal for achieving the highest levels of performance in the five goal areas. The Progress Indicators in the Standards and the language-specific documents outline what is possible when instruction begins in the early grades and continues throughout the secondary years and into postsecondary courses. As more districts begin language learning in elementary grades, it becomes incumbent upon middle school teachers, high school educators, and postsecondary faculty to offer a well-articulated continuation that expands upon student achievement of the Standards. A solid sequence of instruction leads students from novice learners to those with advanced proficiencies.

For a number of reasons, it also will be important for schools to provide multiple entry points into the curriculum. The goal of having students experience the study of world languages every year is not intended to limit the choice of language or the opportunity to begin study of additional languages at predetermined points. Multiple entry points accommodate students who transfer among schools, students who develop interests in specific languages during their middle- or high-school years because of career choices or personal motivation, or students who wish to study additional languages (a concept referred to as "language layering"). In early grades, districts may be able to offer only a limited number of languages due to staffing constraints or the size of schools, but in the middle grades or high school years, provisions for additional languages can be made. Learner choice becomes an increasingly important factor as students mature and their eventual competency is linked with interests and motivation. Students who opt to remain with the study of one world language throughout their K–12 education and beyond will develop high competencies in all the goal areas of the Standards. Students who choose to study more than one world language will reach levels of competency commensurate with the sequence available; their experience with language study in general often contributes to more rapid acquisition of a third language.

HERITAGE LANGUAGE LEARNERS

In many schools around the country, the presence of large groups of students who have home backgrounds in the languages taught at school (e.g., Spanish or Chinese) has led to the establishment of special language courses or programs designed to develop, maintain, and expand the language abilities of these students. In many states, for example, in districts populated by many first, second, and third generation students of Mexican or Central American origin, schools offer both a general language track of Spanish courses as well as a track designed for heritage students, or "Spanish for Spanish Speakers." In dual language programs, classrooms are composed of both native English speakers and learners for whom the second language is their native tongue. Additionally, among many language groups–such as for Arabic, Chinese, or Hindi–the study and learning of heritage languages are supported in community weekend programs and schools.

Specifically, students who enroll in "foreign" language classes are assumed to belong to one of the following two categories: (1) no home background in languages other than English or (2) home background in languages other than English. The latter category can be further divided into those who are speakers of languages commonly taught in schools as world languages (e.g., Spanish); those who are speakers of languages increasingly taught in schools (e.g., Chinese,

Japanese, Russian); and those rarely taught in schools (e.g., Thai, Vietnamese, Hungarian). Among students with home language backgrounds, varying abilities and proficiencies in the heritage language exist. A summary chart of characteristics of home background students is included in Table 1. It illustrates the language development needs facing the language teaching professional with regard to these student characteristics.

Table 1. Characteristics of Home Background Students

STUDENT CHARACTERISTICS	ENGLISH LANGUAGE DEVELOPMENT NEEDS	HERITAGE/HOME LANGUAGE DEVELOPMENT NEEDS
Second and third generation "bilinguals" schooled exclusively in English in the United States	Continued development of age-appropriate English language competencies	Maintenance, retrieval, and/or acquisition of language competencies (e.g., oral productive abilities)

Transfer of literacy skills (reading, listening, viewing) developed in English to the home language

Continued development of age-appropriate competencies in both oral and written modes |
| First generation immigrant students schooled primarily in the United States | Continued development of age-appropriate English language competencies | Development of literacy skills (especially reading) in home language

Continued development of age-appropriate language competencies in oral mode |
| Newly arrived immigrant students | Acquisition of oral and written English | Continued development of age-appropriate competencies in both oral and written modes |

Students with varying needs all require access to language instruction that will allow them to: (1) maintain existing strengths in the language, (2) develop strengths in areas in which the home background has not provided support, and (3) use the language for reading and writing to communicate interpersonally or for a variety of published pieces.

INSTRUCTIONAL APPROACHES

Current research and classroom practices indicate that a variety of approaches can successfully lead learners to competencies in the World-Readiness Standards. The evolving and constantly expanding research base in second language acquisition is identifying effective practices. The best instructional approach for any group of learners ranging from gifted and talented to the challenged learner differs greatly according to factors such as the student's age, home language, learning preferences, and goals for language learning.

What is special about language learning is that it can be learned without formal schooling at all. People "learn" their first languages all over the world without schooling, even without lessons, as might be the case in learning the piano or learning to tap dance. Moreover, this sort of learning is not dependent on talent. While we may say that Mary learned to play the piano "by ear" or José was a "natural artist" from age 4, or that Mei-Ju was a "natural" swimmer at age 5, we do not say that Muhammed had a "real talent" for learning his first language, whereas his brother did not. All children all over the world, unless they have a neurological disorder, are typically fluent in their first language by age 5. They gain control of various components of language for competent use long before the emergence of the cognitive skills that will be necessary for schooled learning and they seemingly learn it "naturally"—that is, without conscious effort. Very young children who learn a second language "naturally" acquire these language skills and abilities at a level appropriate for their age. Older learners, whether in a natural or classroom setting, bring to the process their level of cognitive development as well as their experiences and abilities as skilled users of a first language.

All children are primed to learn languages, and they will rise to meet expectations when goals are appropriately set and the conditions for learning are designed to foster achievement. A learner may be a beginner at any age. Cognitive development is a factor which influences individual progress. For example, when one's first second language experience occurs as a 7-year-old rather than 15-year-old, the instructional approach must recognize differences in motivation, cognitive and motor development, background knowledge, and self-awareness.

Even for older learners, the idea persists today that the best way to learn a language is just to "go to the country" and learn the language "naturally" without formal instruction. Surely, it is rarely said that the best way to learn math is to just "hang around" mathematicians, or the best way to learn studio art is exposure to professional artists, or the best way to learn social studies is to "live in the society." Immersion in country tends to advance proficiency more rapidly when there is a base familiarity with the target language.

Context determines instructional approach as well. If one is learning in an environment where face-to-face interaction with speakers of that language is not available, technology can provide virtual interactions: Skype provides face-to-face communication for students with peers at no additional cost as long as a computer and Internet connection are available. YouTube and other video sources provide sound and sight on a multitude of events of interest to students. Chats and social networking facilitate real-world contact with speakers. Technology works to give learners opportunities to connect with speakers of other languages but it also motivates students to want to learn new languages and cultures. In contrast, in schools and communities where the second language is actively used, teachers can also draw upon such local contexts.

Putting language learning into formal educational environments does not change the features unique to language acquisition; in fact, these features demonstrate that language study is not a sequentially mastered subject matter. Other subject areas that were traditionally taught as a sequence of content are also changing. In mathematics, for example, the school curriculum traditionally moved students through a fairly well-defined sequence of steps in acquiring mathematical competencies involving computation and problem solving, an unfolding of increasingly complex concepts (arithmetic to algebra to calculus) and the learning of a set of facts. Today, the teaching of mathematics is changing to a focus on the larger mathematical practices or habits of mind that create mathematical thinkers prepared to solve unpredictable issues requiring an application of mathematics. Likewise, languages are not "acquired" when students learn an ordered set of facts about the language (e.g., grammar facts, vocabulary). Students need to be able to use the target language for real communication, that is, to carry out a complex interactive process that involves speaking and understanding what others say in the target language, as well as reading, viewing, and interpreting materials in a variety of media. Acquiring communicative competence also involves the acquisition of increasingly complex concepts centering around the relationship between culture and communication. For some learners this acquisition process takes place in a natural setting: They have access to another language because they interact frequently with people who speak to them in this language or because they have spent time abroad. For other students, the process takes place in the classroom. For still others, it takes place in both the classroom and a virtual or real-world setting.

The Standards have been written to suggest that the goals of language learning cannot be divided into a set of sequenced steps. It is not the case that young students must first deal with isolated bits and pieces of language. Real communication is possible for young students as well as for students in secondary and postsecondary institutions. The Standards reflect broad ranges of language proficiency. Differences in cognitive development, maturity, and interests will determine the pace at which learners make progress. The Standards at all levels offer a vision of what learners should know and be able to do in another language.

ORGANIZING PRINCIPLES

This section describes the three major organizing principles used in developing and revising the original Standards for Learning Languages: the broad goals of language instruction, the curricular elements necessary to the attainment of the Standards, and the framework of communicative modes which provides the organizational underpinnings of the Standards.

FIVE Cs OF LEARNING LANGUAGES

The purposes and uses of world languages are as diverse as the learners who study them. Some learners study another language in hopes of finding a rewarding career in the international marketplace or government service. Others are interested in the intellectual challenge and cognitive benefits that accrue to those who develop competency in multiple languages. Still other learners seek greater understanding of other peoples and cultures and see languages as a means of social networking to connect with people around the world. Many learners approach language study, as they do other courses, simply to fulfill a graduation or admissions requirement. Regardless of the reason for study, languages have something to offer to everyone. It is with this philosophy in mind that the Standards Task Force identified five goal areas that encompass all these reasons: Communication, Cultures, Connections, Comparisons, and Communities—5 Cs of language education. ***Communication***, or communicating in languages other than English, is at the heart of second language study, whether the communication takes place face-to-face, virtually, in writing, or through the reading of current events or literature. Through the study of other languages, students gain a knowledge and understanding of the ***cultures*** that use that language; in fact, students cannot truly become proficient in the language until they have also experienced and understood the cultural contexts in which the language occurs. Conversely, one does not truly enter a culture without the ticket provided by its language. Learning languages provides ***connections*** to additional bodies of knowledge that are unavailable to monolingual English speakers. Through ***comparisons*** and contrasts with the language studied, students develop greater insight into their own language and culture and realize that multiple ways of viewing the world exist. Together, these elements enable the student of languages to participate in multilingual ***communities*** at home and around the world in a variety of contexts and in culturally appropriate ways. As is apparent, none of these goals can be separated from the others. Figure 1 illustrates how they interconnect and suggests the richness embodied in human language.

This expanded view of language learning offers particular advantages for the teaching of world languages to all learners. Regardless of educational or career aspirations, language instruction committed to providing experiences in all five goal areas will be beneficial to all learners. Even if learners never speak the language after leaving school, for a lifetime they will retain the cross-cultural skills and knowledge, the insight, and the access to a world beyond traditional borders.

Figure 1. The 5 Cs of Language Study

THE "WEAVE" OF CURRICULAR ELEMENTS

The Standards presented here offer a vision of what learners should know and be able to do with another language. In order to attain these Standards, learners require a language program that provides rich curricular experiences. In the past, classroom instruction was often focused on the memorization of words and grammar rules; the forms of the language were the focus of objectives and instruction. The World-Readiness Standards for Learning Languages require a much broader definition of the content of the language classroom. Learners should be given ample opportunities to explore, develop, and use communication strategies, learning strategies, critical thinking skills, and skills in technology, as well as the appropriate elements of the language system and culture needed to carry out a communicative act. The exact form and content of each of these elements is not prescribed in the present document. Instead, the Standards provide a background, a framework for the reflective teacher to use in weaving these rich curricular experiences into the fabric of language learning. Figure 2 illustrates the correspondence between goal areas of the Standards with content and processes of the curriculum.

Language System

The study of language systems is what most adults typically think of when they remember their second-language learning experience: memorizing dialogues, word lists, grammar rules, verb conjugations, learning new ways of writing, and producing new sounds. These elements are certainly important in the language classroom, but the focus has shifted to using them in terms of the meanings they convey. Being able to recite a verb conjugation is not the same as being able to ask a question or give a piece of information in a comprehensible way in the form required. The language system is a means for attaining the various outcomes described in this document: communicating, gaining cultural understanding, connecting with other disciplines. The language system is also much more than words and rules; it includes the sociolinguistic elements of gestures and other forms of nonverbal communication, of status and discourse style, and "learning what to say to whom and when." These elements form the bridge between language and culture and must be present if students are to learn to interact appropriately in the target language. The specific elements of the language system to be studied within a classroom will naturally vary by language. Some languages, for example, will require students to learn whole new alphabets, while others will present learners with modifications of a few letters. Some languages will have vastly different sentence structures, others will be more familiar. Study of the language system is not the goal or the "end." It is the "means" to successful communication. The language-specific standards provide specialized guidance in this domain.

Figure 2. The "Weave" of Curricular Elements

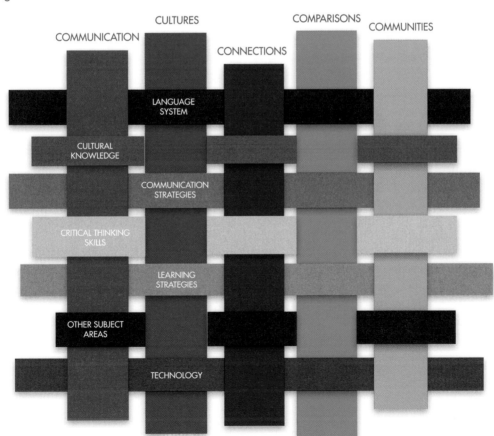

Communication Strategies

Familiarity with the language system alone is not enough to enable learners to engage in successful communicative activities. Learners also must acquire, through specific and focused instruction, the strategies that will aid them in bridging communication gaps that result from differences of language and culture. These communication strategies will empower students as they learn the languages and cultures that they may encounter in the future in their personal lives and careers. These strategies include the ability to: use circumlocution (say things in different ways); guess intelligently (maximize their use of what they know to achieve greater comprehension of what they hear and see); derive meaning from context; understand, interpret, and produce gestures effectively; ask for and provide clarification; make and check hypotheses; make inferences, predictions, and generalizations; reflect on the nature of the interaction; draw informed conclusions; and maintain a healthy sense of humor, patience, and tenacity in the communication process.

Many of these strategies are inherent in some learners; others will have to be taught specifically how to use strategies to interpret meaning and to deliver messages. Therefore, it is essential that educators develop classroom activities that provide learners with ample exposure and practice using those strategies as an integral part of instruction from the very earliest stages of language learning.

Cultural Content

In addition to experience with the language system, learners will need to have access to the richness of the cultures of the languages being studied. They will need to learn about everyday life and social institutions, about contemporary and historical issues that are important in those cultures, about significant works of literature and art, and about cultural attitudes and priorities. Learners should also learn how their own culture is viewed by the people whose language they are studying. Obviously, no single teacher will be able to know everything about the cultures of a given language, nor will every student be able to learn all of those cultural elements. Learners should, however, have access to the tools and learn the communication strategies needed to identify key cultural traits and concepts, and to select, synthesize, and interpret them in ways that result in sensitive and meaningful interaction. Again, the specific elements of culture to be studied will vary by language and even within languages—as is the case, for example, with the many distinct cultures of speakers of Spanish, French, or Arabic.

Learning Strategies

Learning a language requires active mental engagement by the learners. Research shows that effective language learners use specific strategies to enhance their learning, retention, and application of the language. Students can be taught to use these strategies to become more able language learners and to develop a sense of control over their own learning. Teachers can plan direct instruction on learning strategies such as: focusing students' attention on learning; teaching them how to organize in advance by previewing, skimming, or reading for the gist; helping students to reflect on what they have just learned and to summarize; teaching students specific questioning strategies to ask for clarification or explanation; and showing students how to infer information from a text. Students who use learning strategies effectively begin to see themselves as language learners and take on more responsibility for their own progress. Learning strategies benefit all learners since even those who use some strategies effectively can be taught additional ones. Learners are also able to apply effectively these strategies to learning tasks in other disciplines. Broadening the scope of language learning strategies is an integral part of language programs. Learners are able to apply the strategies that work best for them long after they leave the classroom for a lifetime of learning.

Content from Other Subjects

Learners must be given interesting and challenging topics and ideas about which they can read, or that they can discuss or analyze, using their emerging skills with the new language. Many of these topics can be drawn from the wider school curriculum or areas of individual interest. Drawing upon broad curricular content has long been a part of elementary school language classrooms, but is just as valuable in the upper grades and at the university. Teachers who incorporate concepts from science, social studies, mathematics, or music not only enhance the learning of the language but also expand learners' knowledge in other areas. For learners wanting to use the language in furtherance of career or professional purposes, working with content from their disciplines of interest should occur regularly.

Critical Thinking Skills

Starting even at the very early stages and continuing throughout the language learning process, learners engage in a wide variety of critical thinking skills ranging from the basic level of identification and recall to the higher levels of analysis and problem solving. Instruction in the language classroom, as much as in any other discipline, can be designed to promote the use of these skills, and activities can be constructed that incorporate high-level thinking tasks. Students learn to identify the meanings they want to convey for specific communication tasks, select what they already know from their existing body of knowledge, and apply it to new tasks. At the same time, they develop the ability to use a variety of references to seek and incorporate entirely new knowledge in the performance of the tasks. Given a set of cultural issues or problems, they learn to identify, organize, and analyze issues or problems so as to express informed opinions, arrive at informed conclusions, and propose solutions to problems. They can also reflect upon and evaluate the quality and success of their communication so as to strengthen the nature of their interactions in the future. It is also important to remember that learners can use critical thinking skills in beginning language classes by conducting some tasks in English when the target language is not yet available to them in order to deepen their knowledge and understanding and then return to the target language to express these more complex thoughts through the use of various tools and methods (e.g., graphic organizers, guided responses).

Technology

Learners should be given the opportunity during their school careers to take increasing advantage of new technological advances. Access to a variety of technologies ranging from computer-assisted instruction to interactive video, DVDs, the Internet, email, social media, text messages, and apps will help learners strengthen linguistic skills, establish interactions with peers, and learn about contemporary culture and everyday life in the target country. In addition, learners can expand their knowledge of the target culture via edited and unedited programs available on their computers, tablets, or smartphones. Almost every new technology expands the ways in which learners can interact with materials and people using the languages they are learning.

The availability of technology has dramatically changed language classrooms around the country. Teachers and their students have immediate access to authentic materials and to speakers of the language. More traditional media still play a role as learners view films or work with a variety of print sources, including children's literature and publications, magazines, newspapers, literary works, everyday authentic documents (e.g., train schedules, menus, advertisements, maps), and library reference works (e.g., Wikipedia, dictionaries). With Internet versions of print materials and video clips easily translated at the click of a mouse, teachers and learners need to identify appropriate ways to use this technology as a tool to assist with language learning.

THE FRAMEWORK OF COMMUNICATIVE MODES

Researchers from a number of disciplines have worked to understand the nature of language proficiency and to answer the question: What does it mean to "know" a language? (See de Jong & Verhoeven, 1992.) When addressing this question, most introductory textbooks in linguistics (e.g., Fromkin & Rodman, 1993) agree that knowing a language involves the ability to carry out a large variety of tasks in the language. People who know a language speak and are understood by others who know the same language. They know which sounds are in the language and which ones are not; they know that certain sound sequences make up meaningful words; and they are able to combine words to form phrases and phrases to form sentences. They can produce and understand sentences that they have never heard before. Knowing a language means controlling the linguistic system (the syntax, morphology, phonology, semantics, lexis) of a language. It also means being able to access the pragmatic, textual, and sociolinguistic aspects of language, including how to use the language to achieve communicative goals in ways that are appropriate to a particular cultural context (Bachman, 1990; Bialystok, 1981; Canale & Swain, 1980; Hymes, 1985; Savignon, 1983).

Communication can be characterized in many different ways (Schiffrin, 1994). Prior to the Standards, curriculum documents, teachers, and textbooks treated language study in terms of four skills: listening, speaking, reading, writing. The skills paradigm gives an insufficient description of communicative acts. All listening tasks are not the same in terms of conditions, learning processes, or strategies. Listening to a person face-to-face and listening to the news on television are very distinct tasks and require different approaches to teaching, to learning, and to doing. The approach suggested within this document is to recognize three "communicative modes" that place primary emphasis on the context and purpose of the communication (Brecht & Walton, 1994). As illustrated in Table 2, the three modes are: (1) Interpersonal, (2) Interpretive, and (3) Presentational. Each mode involves a particular link between language and the underlying culture that is developed gradually over time.

The Interpersonal Mode. The Interpersonal Mode is characterized by active negotiation of meaning among individuals. Participants observe and monitor one another to see how their meanings and intentions are being communicated. Adjustments and clarifications can be made accordingly. As a result, there is a higher probability of ultimately achieving the goal of successful communication in this mode than in the other two modes. The Interpersonal Mode is most obvious in conversation, but both the interpersonal and negotiated dimensions can be realized through reading and writing, such as the exchange of text messages, online chats, or in wikis or moodles, where negotiated meanings can occur.

Table 2. Framework of Communicative Modes

	INTERPERSONAL	INTERPRETIVE	PRESENTATIONAL
DEFINITIONS	Direct oral communication (e.g., face-to-face or telephonic) between individuals who are in personal contact Direct written communication between individuals who come into personal contact	Receptive communication of oral or written messages Mediated communication via print and non-print materials Listener, viewer, reader works with visual or recorded materials whose creator is absent	Productive communication using oral or written language Spoken or written communication for people (an audience) with whom there is no immediate personal contact or which takes place in a one-to-many mode Author or creator of visual or recorded material not known personally to listener or reader
PATHS	Productive abilities: speaking, writing Receptive abilities: listening, reading	Primarily receptive abilities: listening, reading, viewing	Primarily productive abilities: speaking, writing, showing
CULTURAL KNOWLEDGE	Knowledge of cultural perspectives governing interactions between individuals of different ages, statuses, backgrounds Ability to recognize that languages use different practices to communicate Ability to recognize that cultures use different patterns of inter-action	Knowledge of how cultural perspectives are embedded in products (literary and artistic) Knowledge of how meaning is encoded in products Ability to analyze content, compare it to information available in first language, and assess linguistic and cultural differences Ability to analyze and compare content in one culture to interpret U.S. culture	Knowledge of cultural perspectives governing interactions between a speaker and his/her audience and a writer and his/her reader Ability to present cross-cultural information based on background of the audience Ability to recognize that cultures use different patterns of inter-action
KNOWLEDGE OF THE LINGUISTIC SYSTEM			
The use of grammatical, lexical, phonological, semantic, pragmatic, and discourse features necessary for participation in the three communicative modes.			

The Interpretive Mode. The Interpretive Mode is focused on the appropriate cultural interpretation of meanings that occur in written, spoken, or visual form where there is no recourse to the active negotiation of meaning with the writer, speaker, or producer of the message. Such instances of "one-way" reading, listening, or viewing include the interpretation of web pages, literary texts, movies, radio and television broadcasts, video clips, and podcasts. Interpreting the cultural meaning of texts, oral or written, must be distinguished from the notion of reading and listening "comprehension," where the term could refer to understanding a text from the reader's or listener's perspective. Put another way, interpretation differs from comprehension in that the former implies the ability to "read (listen or view) between the lines."

Since the Interpretive Mode does not allow for active negotiation between the reader and the writer, the listener and the speaker, or the viewer and the producer, it requires a much more profound knowledge of culture from the outset. The more one knows about the other language and culture, the greater the chances of creating the appropriate cultural interpretation of a written, spoken, or visual text. It must be noted, however, that cultural literacy and the ability to read, listen, or view between the lines are developed over time and through exposure to the language and culture.

The Presentational Mode. The Presentational Mode refers to the creation of messages in a manner that facilitates interpretation by members of the other culture where no direct opportunity for the active negotiation of meaning between members of the two cultures exists. Examples include the writing of reports and articles or the presentation of speeches or videos. These examples of "one-way" writing, speaking, and visually representing require a substantial knowledge of language and culture from the outset, since the goal is to make sure that members of the other culture, the audience, will be successful in reading and listening between the lines. In the classroom, a presentational task requires that students draft and revise the publication or talk so that it succeeds in conveying the message as intended. It differs greatly from interpersonal communication where understandings can be worked through in a face-to-face setting or through instant interaction via technology.

The Communicative Framework and the Background of the Learner

This framework is useful, whether discussing the language abilities of students with home background in languages other than English, beginning language students, or those at an advanced level. Heritage language learners may bring strong interpersonal communication skills in the target/home language, but they may still need to develop the ability to use the language in both the Interpretive and Presentational Modes. The varying needs of learners require access to instruction that will allow them to: (1) maintain existing strengths in the language; (2) develop strengths in topical areas in which the home background has not provided support; and (3) use the language for reading and writing.

The five goals of language education presented here, then, are as important to home or heritage language speakers as they are to learners beginning and continuing the study of language exclusively in a classroom setting. Specifically, home background students who study their first language as an academic subject at school can profit significantly from instruction that is focused on the goals and standards presented in this document: (1) expanding their communicative abilities; (2) offering them the opportunity to gain knowledge of the several cultures and national groups that speak their heritage language; (3) using their home language in an academic context to access new information and knowledge; (4) bringing to the level of awareness the views and perspectives of the two worlds with which they interact on a daily basis; and (5) expanding their ability to participate both in the United States and abroad as members of a language competent society.

The Communicative Framework and the Nature of the Language Being Studied

The use of a framework of communicative modes also highlights the challenge to native speakers of English who study non-European languages or those with a non-Roman alphabet or logographic writing system (such as Chinese) or a visual language (such as American Sign Language). Cultural distance will place great demands on the Interpersonal negotiated mode, because the process of negotiation requires abilities that will be unfamiliar to the typical speaker of a European language. Likewise, the amount of cultural knowledge ultimately required for the Interpretive and Presentational Modes is presumably much greater for native speakers of a European language studying non-European languages than for students of one European language (e.g., English) studying another European language (e.g., Italian). We expect that the Interpretive Mode would predominate in the study of classical languages such as Latin, perhaps with some attention to the Presentational and Interpersonal mode as a way of strengthening language knowledge and use. Some attention may be given to the oral dimension in classical languages, mainly as a successful learning tool to build fluency as the learner needs to comprehend and respond in real time and by focusing on phrases and overall meaning rather than each individual word in isolation.

Planning for Language Learning

These organizing principles are intended to guide the development of language learning programs, curriculum, instruction, and assessment. These principles describe the complexity of learning languages and outline the critical elements that need to be woven throughout language learning, incorporating a balance of the 5 Cs (the Goal Areas of the Standards), the weave of curricular elements, and the constant connection with the modes of communication. The World-Readiness Standards for Learning Languages make explicit the link of language with meaningful content, not only with the three Communication Standards, but also by emphasizing "use the language" in seven of the other eight Standards. The Standards outline learning goals with the flexibility to be adaptable to learners of any age, any grade, any background, any institution or instructional setting, and any language.

The World-Readiness Standards for Learning Languages were written with a variety of audiences in mind: pre-K–16 language teachers and teacher educators, curriculum writers, administrators, policy makers at all levels of government, parents, and business and community leaders. The goal of this document is to describe for all of these audiences what learners of languages should know and be able to do at the end of high school or college or a sequence of study; it does not prescribe how leaners should reach specific outcomes. Rather, it offers guidance to those responsible for assisting them on the journey.

ORGANIZATION AND DEFINITIONS

The World-Readiness Standards for Learning Languages are organized within the five *Goal Areas* which make up language education: *Communication, Cultures, Connections, Comparisons,* and *Communities.* None of these goals stands alone; all are interconnected. Each goal area contains a rationale for its inclusion as a part of language education and a discussion of definitions and important pedagogical issues associated with it. Table 3 provides an overview to the organization of the Standards.

Each goal area contains two to three **Content Standards**. These Standards describe the knowledge and abilities that all students should acquire as they progress through the language sequence. Each Standard is followed by a brief discussion to further explicate and illustrate the Standard and to define its place within the goal area.

For the goal area of Communication, **Performance Descriptors** provide an overview to how well learners are able to use language as they improve their performance, moving from the Novice range to the Intermediate range and into the Advanced range. These Performance Descriptors are from the *ACTFL Performance Descriptors for Language Learners* (2012a), integrating that description of performance for the modes of communication with this guide to implementing the Standards.

Under the Communication Standards for the Interpersonal and Presentational Modes are **Sample Performance Indicators** for Novice, Intermediate, Advanced, and Superior ranges; they define observable student outcomes in meeting the Standards, but are not themselves Standards. The Sample Performance Indicators are from the *NCSSFL-ACTFL Can-Do Statements* (2013) and are appropriately integrated to illustrate learning targets for the Interpersonal and Presentational Modes. The unique nature of the Interpretive Mode for second language learners is explained in the chapter on the Goal Area of Communication: The Interpretive Mode does not develop in the same sequence as the productive communication skills (Interpersonal and Presentational Modes), as it is strongly influenced by the learner's first language literacy strategies. The Sample Performance Indicators are neither prescriptive nor exhaustive; they are examples of student performances at those levels but some accommodation must be made for the age of the learner. They can realistically be achieved at some level by all students and allow for a variety of content to demonstrate the indicator. Sample Performance Indicators provide for a multitude of instructional possibilities and are to be interpreted by curriculum developers and classroom teachers who will transform them into classroom practice. They are measurable and assessable in numerous ways and are designed for use by states, districts, or departments to establish acceptable performance levels for their students.

Following the Sample Performance Indicators are **Sample Progress Indicators** for each of the three modes of communication. These tasks are examples for the Novice, Intermediate, and Advanced ranges of performance. Rather than being tied to specific grade levels, the Sample Progress Indicators are appropriate for learners of any age who are at the targeted level of language. Educators need to remember that Novice, Intermediate, and Advanced refer to language performance, not to the age of the learners, and these sample tasks should be adapted to content that is motivating and engaging to the learners, given their age, experiences, and interests. The language-specific standards provide examples tied directly to content and tasks that incorporate specific topics and language competencies for that language.

For the other four goal areas (Cultures, Connections, Comparisons, and Communities), following each standard are the **Sample Progress Indicators**. These Sample Progress Indicators are examples of what learners at different performance levels (Novice, Intermediate, and Advanced) do to demonstrate the knowledge and skill of that Standard using the language. Learners at the Novice range of language performance are not at a simple level of thinking and may be in elementary grades, middle school, high school, or a postsecondary institution. It is not the thinking behind the task that signals Novice, Intermediate, or Advanced; it is the language the learner is able to use to investigate, explain, or reflect on the content that makes it appropriate for a specific language level. For that reason, each performance range may be illustrated with tasks generic to the range (e.g., Intermediate learners), and also by tasks specific to the age/grade of the learners (e.g., Intermediate learners in elementary grades, Intermediate learners in middle school and high school, and Intermediate learners at the postsecondary level).

Table 3. Overview to Components of the Standards

get your head wrapped around

FOR COMMUNICATION	
COMPONENT	**EXAMPLE**
Goal Area:	Communication (p. 43)
Short descriptive phrase of the goal area	Communicate effectively in more than one language in order to function in a variety of situations and for multiple purposes (p. 43)
Title for Standard:	Interpersonal Communication (p. 50)
Content Standard:	Learners interact and negotiate meaning in spoken, signed, or written conversations to share information, reactions, feelings, and opinions. (p. 50)
Performance Descriptors • Novice • Intermediate • Advanced	Intermediate Range (p. 51): Expresses self and participates in conversations on familiar topics using sentences and series of sentences. Handles short social interactions in everyday situations by asking and answering a variety of questions. Can communicate about self, others, and everyday life.
Sample Performance Indicators • Novice Low-Mid-High • Intermediate Low-Mid-High • Advanced Low-Mid-High • Superior	Global Statement—Sample Indicators (p. 52)

	Intermediate Low Learners can participate in conversations on a number of familiar topics using simple sentences. They can handle short social interactions in everyday situations by asking and answering simple questions.	**Intermediate Low Learners can** • have a simple conversation on a number of everyday topics • ask and answer questions on factual information that is familiar to them • use the language to meet their basic needs in familiar situations

Sample Progress Indicators	Sample Tasks (p. 54) • Novice Range • Intermediate Range – Students exchange information about personal events, memorable experiences, and other school subjects with peers and/or members of the target cultures. • Advanced Range

FOR CULTURES, CONNECTIONS, COMPARISONS, AND COMMUNITIES	
COMPONENT	**EXAMPLE**
Goal Area:	Cultures (p. 67)
Short descriptive phrase of the goal area	Interact with cultural competence and understanding (p. 67)
Title for Standard:	Relating Cultural Practices to Perspectives (p. 72)
Standard:	Learners use the language to investigate, explain, and reflect on the relationship between the practices and perspectives of the cultures studied. (p. 72)
Sample Progress Indicators	Novice Range Learners (p. 73) • Novice Learners • Novice Learners in Elementary School • Novice Learners in Middle School and High School • Novice Learners at the Postsecondary Level Intermediate Range Learners (p. 74) • Intermediate Learners • Intermediate Learners in Elementary School • Intermediate Learners in Middle School and High School • Intermediate Learners at the Postsecondary Level Advanced Range Learners (p. 75) • Advanced Learners • Advanced Learners in Middle School and High School • Advanced Learners at the Postsecondary Level

Relationship to the ACTFL Proficiency Guidelines

In 1986, ACTFL released the ACTFL Proficiency Guidelines. Based on the scale developed for use by the federal government, the Guidelines provided a common metric against which to measure performance in speaking, reading, writing, and listening in a second language. The work on proficiency provided the profession with a common yardstick with which to begin the discussion of performance assessment especially of speaking and writing. These discussions have placed the language profession in an excellent position to develop new kinds of performance-based assessments that reflect the Standards in this document. It is obvious however in working with the Standards that they encompass much more than the separate skills format outlined in the Proficiency Guidelines.

Teachers will recognize the influence of the Guidelines within the Standards, particularly in the area of communication. The Standards go beyond proficiency at the skill level, however. The effort to create broadly conceived standards that reflect current thinking means that communication is organized around the framework of Interpersonal, Interpretive, and Presentational modes, rather than carved into separate skill areas of listening, speaking, reading, and writing.

This reflects research in second language acquisition that has grown as a field of inquiry since the Proficiency Guidelines. In 1998, ACTFL issued its Performance Guidelines for K–12 Learners. These are performance standards that define the "how well" students can be expected to do the "what" from the content standards. The K–12 Performance Guidelines–revised in 2012 and renamed the Performance Descriptors for Language Learners–set forth characteristics of language users at the various stages or benchmarks of learning and development and are articulated according to the communicative modes: Interpersonal, Interpretive, and Presentational.

The Performance Descriptors for Language Learners connect language learning with a broader development of literacy in the learners' first and second languages. The Performance Descriptors include communication strategies and cultural awareness as two of the important domains to mark progress along the continuum from Novice to Intermediate and on to Advanced. The World-Readiness Standards make even more explicit the link of literacy with the development of 21st century skills that include information, technology, and media literacy along with an emphasis on communication, collaboration, creativity, and critical thinking.

Setting Performance Standards for Language Competencies

Individual states and school districts hold the responsibility for determining performance standards for their students. At the same time, the Standards document was developed in the context of raising U.S. expectations to those of schools in other nations and matching students' desire to use language for personal and career purposes where engagement with people and cultures require real world competencies. The Sample Performance Indicators of this Standards document provide an outline of what learners will be able to do with the language, framed as statements of what learners will be able to say they "can do." Sample tasks for assessing these targeted performances are found in the Sample Progress Indicators.

In a language program based on the Standards outlined in this document, assessment needs to focus on language performance. The Integrated Performance Assessment (IPA) model is appropriate for gathering evidence of what learners "can do" with language. This summative assessment model connects tasks in each of the three modes, providing learners with a motivating application of the skills and knowledge they have acquired, and demonstrating that application through a task in each mode of communication. The Sample Performance Indicators (from the NCSSFL-ACTFL Can-Do Statements) provide examples that learners and educators alike can use for goal-setting and to guide self-assessment, charting learners' improvement and progress.

Particularly for the extended sequences of study envisioned in this document, it will be important that schools set exit standards for communication that reflect the additional time available as well as the range of goals outlined in the World-Readiness Standards. All students with motivation and opportunity to learn should be able to reach a stage that reflects abilities to create with the language, to function effectively in that language in anticipated and expanded contexts, to be flexible enough to negotiate meanings on a variety of topics, to pick up a magazine or book, pull up a website or video that appeals to their age and interests and understand portions of it, and to behave in culturally acceptable ways. All learners can excel and advance to a stage where their language allows them to have greater choice and control in using language to accomplish a variety of purposes in a wide range of situations.

HOW TO USE THIS DOCUMENT

This new edition of *World-Readiness Standards for Learning Languages* is a document designed for many audiences and with many purposes. Before using this document, however, it is important to understand what it is not. First and foremost, the Standards reflect best practices and describe what is being attained by students in programs built upon the Standards since their release in 1996. The Standards described within these pages will not be achieved overnight; rather, they provide a gauge against which to measure gains in language education. Surveys conducted in 2010 indicate that much progress is being made toward these Standards, but there is much still to be done (Phillips & Abbott, 2011).

The Standards are not a curriculum guide. While this document suggests the types of content and curricular experiences needed to enable learners to achieve the Standards and supports the ideal of extended sequences of study, it does not describe specific course content, nor a recommended scope and sequence.

Finally, this is not a stand-alone document. It must be used in conjunction with state and local frameworks and standards to determine the best approaches and reasonable expectations for the learners in individual districts and schools. As Figure 3 indicates, each of these documents will influence and inform the others, as administrators, educators, parents, and others work together to ensure that tomorrow's learners are equipped to function in an ever-shrinking world. In higher education, programs can use the Standards to define outcomes for courses and to design paths of language study in conjunction with other disciplines and for teacher education.

Figure 3. The Relationships Among National, State, and Local Standards Documents

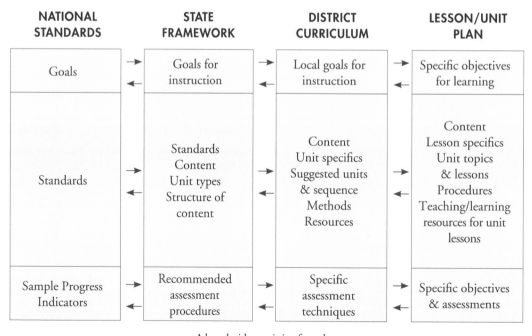

Adapted with permission from the
Visual Arts Education Reform Handbook: Suggested Policy Perspectives on Art Content and Student Learning in Art Education
National Art Education Association, 1995

Standards and Specific Languages

This volume discusses the Standards from a broad perspective that applies to all languages. Available with this volume is access to language-specific standards devoted to learning American Sign Language (ASL), Arabic, Chinese, Classical Languages, French, German, Hindi, Italian, Japanese, Korean, Portuguese, Russian, Scandinavian Languages, and Spanish. Other languages will be added as professionals create their own standards alignment. These specific standards for additional languages may be accessed once they are developed and finalized. The language-specific standards adjust for the differences among languages: Each language has distinct vocabulary, syntactic structures, sound systems, writing systems, and cultures to be addressed. Each offers greater and lesser challenges to English-speaking students. In that the common goals and actual standards represent the consensus of the field as to overall objectives of second-language study, they are stable.

The Sample Progress Indicators, however, are much more fluid. Native English-speaking learners of languages with non-Roman alphabets, for example, may need a longer time to reach some of the Progress Indicators for written language than do students of a language closely related to English. Students of some languages may need more time to progress from the Novice to Intermediate range. Written literacy may develop more slowly when a non-Roman alphabet or non-alphabetic writing system is used. Conversely, the cultural differences embedded in the study of non-European languages may be more readily apparent than the cultural differences in European languages. Similar challenges exist when working with visual languages (e.g., American Sign Language), languages no longer spoken as a native language (e.g., Latin and Ancient Greek), and languages with no written system (e.g., some Native American languages).

The language-specific standards discuss why students might want to learn that language in terms of its importance in literature, business, international exchange, presence in the United States both historically and currently, and other compelling reasons. Most importantly, these provide learning scenarios to assist teachers in making the transition to standards-oriented curricula. The scenarios are based upon actual classroom activities submitted by educators to the language-specific writing groups. Each scenario includes a list of the targeted Standards, a description of the activity as it plays out in the classroom where it was used, and a reflection on how it addressed the Standards. Many scenarios also suggest modifications for different age or learning levels. For the most part, educators tend to read and study the Standards for the languages they teach; they are encouraged, however, to read across languages since many useful ideas and examples can be adapted for their own lessons.

Standards and Heritage Language Learners

Similar modifications in Progress Indicators and emphasis on Standards will need to be made when applying the Standards to learners who have a home background in the language studied. As stated previously, these students may come to class able to converse in the language in home and community situations but may lack the abilities to interact comfortably in more formal settings. Further, they may be quite comfortable with oral language but possess limited skills in reading and writing. They may know well the traditions of one culture where the language is used but have limited familiarity with other cultures in that same language family. Again, the background of the learner is an important variable when developing implementation strategies for these Standards.

WORLD-READINESS STANDARDS FOR LEARNING LANGUAGES

GOAL AREA: COMMUNICATION

Communicate effectively in more than one language in order to function in a variety of situations and for multiple purposes

RATIONALE

For American students, the ability to function competently in at least one language other than English is vital for success in the interconnected world of the 21st century. Effective communication and collaboration in another language, including the ability to function appropriately with and within other cultures, are critical components in preparing learners for college, career, and world readiness. Global economies not limited to national borders, heightened needs for national security, and rapidly changing demographics within the United States all require students from elementary school through postsecondary education to develop skills in one or more world languages and the respective cultures. In today's world, language competence requires much more than simply being able to talk about the language and its culture(s), describe its grammatical structures, or conjugate verbs and memorize lists of vocabulary. Twenty-first century learners must be able to comprehend both spoken and written language in multiple contexts in order to access information and engage in collaboration in any field. They must be able to think and interact in a global community by participating appropriately in face-to-face interaction in physical or virtual environments with members of other societies, and by interpreting and analyzing the concepts, ideas, and opinions expressed by members of these societies through their media and their literatures.

Communicating in another language provides another avenue for students to become critical thinkers, good problem solvers, and informed, productive global citizens.

DISCUSSION

Successful communication in another language requires learners to develop facility with the language, familiarity with the cultures of the speakers who use the language, and an understanding of how language and culture interact in societies around the globe. With an ultimate goal of creating lifelong, responsible global citizens, learners must apply these skills and knowledge as they express and interpret events and ideas in another language both within and beyond the classroom, reflect upon observations of and interactions with other cultures, make connections with other disciplines, and make comparisons with their own languages and cultures. Thus, achieving the Standards in the Communication goal is central to the attainment of all the other Standards.

In order to develop intercultural communicative competence, learners must understand how interpersonal interactions are conducted in the cultures in which the target language is spoken, how individuals use language effectively to achieve different purposes, how discourse conventions work, how oral and written texts are structured, and how the language system operates. Learners must weave this knowledge together in the process of transmitting and receiving meaningful messages, while at the same time interacting using behaviors that are culturally appropriate. The Council of Europe in the Common European Framework describes "interculturality" as the ability to bring the culture of origin and the foreign culture into relation with each other, involving cultural sensitivity and the ability to identify and use a variety of strategies to interact with people from other cultures, the capacity to be an intermediary between one's own culture and the foreign culture, the ability to deal effectively with intercultural misunderstanding and conflict, and the ability to overcome stereotyped relationships. (Council of Europe, pp. 104-105) Language and culture are inseparable and are at the heart of communication.

In order to achieve the Communication Standards, learners must have ample opportunities to experience the world language as it is spoken and written in the target cultures. Meaningful, authentic language from real contexts becomes the basis for the development of expression and creativity in another language. People who grow up in different cultures acquire their first language in a particular cultural context; they must learn comparable cultural constructs and behaviors to communicative effectively in newly acquired languages. It is essential that learners be surrounded with interesting and age-appropriate materials as a basis for acquiring a new language system in its cultural contexts so that they are able to communicate effectively in the language. Language educators at all levels should use the language as a vehicle to increase learners' knowledge and understanding of the world.

GUIDING LEARNERS TO IMPROVE LANGUAGE PERFORMANCE

Standards are intended to influence curriculum, learning tasks, teaching approaches, course outcomes, and measurement of student progress over time. The World-Readiness Standards for Learning Languages are meant to guide effective language learning. The Standards guide learning in an instructional setting, be it a classroom, a virtual learning environment, working with a tutor, or coached independent study. Through the coaching of an instructor or the guidance of instructional materials, learners develop their language performance by learning and practicing language functions, structures, and vocabulary in contexts that reflect authentic, real-world use of language.

As opposed to long-held beliefs, we now know that students do not acquire an intercultural communicative competence by first learning the elements of the language system prior to putting them together to convey a message. It is not the case that learners learn best by memorizing vocabulary items in isolation and by producing limited simple sentences. Even those students who learn grammar easily and well and are able to pass tests on nouns, verb conjugations, tense usage, and the like may be quite unable to understand language when it is spoken to them or respond appropriately if grammatical concepts have been learned outside of any functional context. The study of the language system itself, while useful for some learners, does not automatically result in the development of the ability to process language in real situations and in the ability to respond meaningfully in appropriate ways.

Performance and proficiency are two words used frequently to describe the language that learners produce; however, they are not the same thing. Language performance is based on instruction: The language learner demonstrates what was learned. Performance is practiced, initially in more controlled ways. Gradually, the responsibility is shifted from instructor to learner so performance can become increasingly independent of the instructor's guidance or prompts. The content for language performance is familiar, based on what was learned, practiced, or rehearsed, and then applied to a new setting; likewise, the context for language performance is familiar. By contrast, language proficiency is independent of specific instruction or curriculum. Assessment of language proficiency does not take into consideration where, when, or how language was acquired. An assessment of proficiency involves non-rehearsed situations and tasks, stretching to demonstrate control of language to handle the content and contexts appropriate for a given level. Language performance points toward proficiency by providing evidence of how the learner would be rated on an assessment of proficiency. Multiple measures of language performance over time are needed to provide a sense of the language learner's likely proficiency level. (ACTFL, 2012a, pp. 4–5)

Language performance can be guided, coached, or practiced. Instructors carefully create scaffolded learning tasks, that is, they design activities to support and help learners understand and express more in the language than they could do on their own. In order to move to higher levels of language performance, instructors need to provide tasks that help learners produce or understand language at the next higher level. For example, beginning language learners acquire memorized vocabulary which they can use to replace elements in memorized sentence patterns, using the memorized structure to express personal meaning, which might look like providing learners with the sentence pattern: "I like to _____ because I'm interested in _____." Learners would express personal meaning by filling in the first blank with a leisure time activity and the second blank with things they like about that activity. In this example, the instructor has created a scaffolded task to help learners at the Novice range of performance communicate like learners at the Intermediate range, able to produce original sentences. In this way, instructors help learners converse, narrate, request, explain, argue, criticize, or persuade, using the language they have internalized to communicate effectively.

Learners often bring insights that they have obtained from having developed proficiency in their first language to the study of a second one. They know how to request personal information from others, how to describe, how to persuade, and how to explain. Depending on their age and literacy development, learners are able to obtain a certain amount of information from texts and media and to interpret that information. When they do learn a second language, then, they bring a certain degree of prior knowledge and skill about how to transmit and express meanings. However, they must learn how to do so by using a different language system and by following what may be a very different set of implicit or explicit rules.

We know that learners improve when they are provided multiple opportunities to use the target language to communicate in a variety of situations and for multiple purposes. The more learners use the language in meaningful situations, the more rapidly they move to higher levels of language performance. Active and constructive use of language is central to the learning process; therefore, learners must be involved in generating both oral and written language for their ideas, moving from simple words, phrases, and sentences to more complex phrases, sentences, and paragraphs as they progress from one level of proficiency to the next. They learn by doing, by trying out language, by taking risks with it, by receiving interactive feedback, and by modifying their language to serve their communicative needs, depending on the nature of their interactions and their audience. Regardless of their stage of language acquisition, learners require strategies that allow them to compensate for language that they have not yet internalized. These strategies include, but are not limited to, requesting clarification, focusing on key words and phrases, monitoring their own and others' performance, using inductive and deductive reasoning, practicing sounds and structures subvocally or aloud, using various mnemonic techniques, and using nonverbal communication strategies.

To support learners as they try to make meaning of what they hear, read, or view or to express meaning as they speak, write, or represent visually, instructors need to use a variety of strategies, including:
- providing comprehensible input that is directed toward communicative goals;
- making meaning clear through body language, gestures, and visual support;
- conducting comprehension checks to ensure understanding;
- negotiating meaning with learners and encouraging negotiation among learners;
- eliciting expression that increases in fluency, accuracy, and complexity over time;
- encouraging self-expression and spontaneous use of language;
- teaching learners strategies for requesting clarification and assistance when faced with comprehension difficulties; and
- offering feedback to assist and improve learners' ability to interact, create messages, and understand messages in the target language. (Use of the Target Language in the Classroom Position Statement, ACTFL, 2012b).

Communication Standards

STANDARDS

C Interpersonal Communication

C Interpretive Communication

C Presentational Communication

The Communication goal includes three Standards based on the Framework of Communicative Modes (pp. 32–34). These Standards focus on the purpose behind the communication more than the means. Interpersonal communication focuses on exchanging information, reactions, feelings, and opinions by negotiating and clarifying meaning. The key focus in interpretive communication is to answer the question: "What does the author, speaker, or producer of media want you to understand?" Presentational communication is used to create a message for a specific purpose and for a specific audience. With the initial publication of *National Standards for Foreign Language Learning: Preparing for the 21st Century* in 1996, the designation of modes of communication was a dramatic shift from past practice of identifying language in terms of four skills: reading, writing, listening, and speaking—a model that dominated language teaching, learning, and assessment for decades. The emphasis on four skills did not historically take into consideration the context of communication. A four-skills approach assumes that "listening is listening is listening"—although we know that this is not how communication occurs in real life. Listening to a person face-to-face or in an online video chat and exchanging information is quite different from listening to a menu of options in a phone call, and that in turn is different from accessing the message from a video clip online. In the Interpersonal Mode, if you are listening to another person and do not understand, you can ask for clarification or for the person to repeat or to say it another way. As a listener, you can negotiate meaning with the individual; you use a host of strategies to reach understanding. When faced with a recorded menu of options in a phone call that you don't understand right away, you might press the number that repeats the options, or press "0" in hopes of connecting to a human voice. In the example of the video clip, you use the actions, emotions, and cultural clues that you see; you replay the segment; and you do some thinking, guessing and hypothesizing to figure out what is occurring and what your reaction or response might be.

The consideration of the modes provides important insights for teaching and learning that connect with the current nationwide discussion of literacy. Literacy as described in individual states' standards, or in the Common Core State Standards, is often divided into the four skills (reading, writing, listening, and speaking), and language (being attentive to the conventions of the language, using increasingly precise vocabulary, and understanding how language functions). The World-Readiness Standards for Learning Languages support these same elements by emphasizing the purpose behind the communication: situations where listening may be done for interpretive communication, or when it is combined with speaking for interpersonal communication. Likewise, writing may be for presentational communication, or when it is combined with reading, it could be for interpersonal communication—as in text messaging. Clearly, different means are required to develop, practice, and assess these skills depending on the communicative purpose behind them. In this way, the modes of communication provide additional insights for developing learners' literacy whether in their first or second language.

This shift from four skills to three modes has an important influence on curriculum, instruction, and assessment. Just as the communicative modes play out differently for the student at any age or level of language learning, they also require the teacher to vary the instructional approaches chosen to develop and to assess them. The survey of teachers about their implementation of the Standards (Phillips & Abbott, 2011) indicates that many do build lessons around interpersonal, interpretive, or presentational communication but some still describe activities in terms of skills alone. The modes enable teachers to ensure that communication is developed in purposeful ways and in the contexts in which it occurs in the real world, including the use of authentic resources. Identifying an activity or assessment task by its mode—that is, the communicative purpose behind the task—gives educators and learners more direction as to the goal for the task, than by simply labeling the task as "listening comprehension" or "writing." For example, while providing learners with a script to memorize may be a way to practice speaking skills, thinking through the lens of the modes of communication will lead educators to design different types of tasks. If the focus is on the Presentational Mode, learners will be guided to create, practice, and memorize a written skit from a chosen set of materials and perform it for their classmates. If the focus is on the Interpersonal Mode, learners will be placed in scenarios in which they will need to spontaneously interact and negotiate meaning in order to accomplish the task, such as looking at three menus and coming to agreement on which one has the healthiest options for that night's dinner.

Another important aspect of the Communication goal is that the three Standards support one another in the development of the learner's language performance. For each of the modes of communication (Interpersonal, Interpretive, and Presentational), learning activities in one mode often link to or build on activities in another mode. When learners have spontaneous interpersonal conversations, one of the most difficult aspects is having something to talk about. If the topic is one with which the learners are not familiar, such as comparing their own community or school to one in another culture, an authentic document can provide content and even vocabulary to draw upon for the conversation. Rather than having to imagine cultural similarities or differences comparing their school to one abroad, learners will have much more to talk about if they are looking at a school website from a country where the language is spoken: The Interpretive Mode is providing content for the Interpersonal Mode activity to be more successful, let alone more motivating. Another example would be asking learners to first discuss with a conversation partner what they feel are the key points from an article representing one side of a debate topic and then to individually write down a summary of the most convincing evidence that shaped their opinion on the topic: The Interpretive Mode was a catalyst for an activity in the Interpersonal Mode, which prepared learners to be more successful in the output of the Presentational Mode. In assessment, it is important to know which mode is being assessed and not to use evidence from one mode as evidence of another mode. For example, asking learners to produce language to show that they understood language will not allow the instructor to know where their confusion was. In the classroom, the instructor is there to support and guide learners if confusion arises, and the modes work together to increase language performance, support multiple means to explore a topic, and motivate learners with more than one way to understand and express meaning.

It should be emphasized that while the Communication goal is central to the achievement of all other goal areas, it cannot be viewed in isolation. Learners need a variety of learning experiences in the other goal areas, integrated with Communication, in order to have content worth communicating. The World-Readiness Standards for Learning Languages include the words "use the language" in each of the other four goal areas: Cultures, Connections, Comparisons, and Communities. This reinforces the link of learning to communicate with content to explore. Rather than treating the language itself as the content to explore, the content for learning, practicing, and assessing Communication comes from the practices, products, and perspectives of Cultures, the critical thinking and problem solving around information and diverse perspectives of Connections, the insights around language and culture described in Comparisons, and the interaction with multilingual communities and setting of goals of Communities.

C INTERPERSONAL COMMUNICATION

Learners interact and negotiate meaning in spoken, signed, or written conversations to share information, reactions, feelings, and opinions.

This Standard focuses on interpersonal (i.e., two-way) communication including listening and speaking in a conversation, exchanging communication through American Sign Language (ASL), and reading and writing as in a text message. Interpersonal communication, may occur face-to-face or in a virtual environment, for example, a chat room, a Google hangout, or using a software application such as Skype. Smartphones and other electronic devices allow instant access to a multitude of social networking sites (e.g., Twitter, Facebook, and LinkedIn) as well as to interpersonal communication via text messaging, email, and photo/video sharing. Interpersonal communication is also spontaneous, not rehearsed, and involves the interaction between conversational partners that may often go in unpredictable directions. Interpersonal communication involves the negotiation of meaning when conversational partners do not understand each other. Interpersonal communication relies on strategies such as asking for clarification (e.g., Huh?, Please repeat that, Do you mean to say that . . . ?), circumlocution (using words the speaker does know to describe the word or words the speaker does not know), and using gestures and facial expressions to help communicate the message. Interpersonal communication may be informal, such as two friends having a video chat, or formal, such as two people collaborating on a project.

Students can learn oral, written, and nonverbal communication skills from the very beginning that permit them to interact with each other and to focus primarily on the message. While the message is the main focus in interpersonal communication, this does not mean that accuracy has no importance. The difference in two-way communication is that while accuracy does move the conversation along more efficiently, the people exchanging messages can use various means to negotiate meaning when there is a breakdown in communication or a lack of understanding due to inaccurate vocabulary or grammatical structures. The message to learners is not that accuracy does not matter, but rather that one should use all strategies available to understand and be understood. Learners who only focus on accuracy often remain in the Novice range because they may rarely stretch to create with language or practice sufficiently moving beyond purely memorized language. During the course of their language learning, learners need to practice these skills in a variety of forms and contexts so that their interactions occur in an increasingly accurate and culturally appropriate manner. Learners who come with a home background in the language may have already acquired such abilities to a certain extent.

The Continuum of Language Performance in the Interpersonal Mode

To guide curriculum, instruction, and assessment, this document connects the Communication Standards with two useful descriptions of language performance: the Performance Descriptors for Language Learners (ACTFL, 2012a) and the NCSSFL-ACTFL Can-Do Statements (2013).

The Performance Descriptors describe the range of performance that is the result of instruction in an instructional setting. The performance is described for three levels: Novice, Intermediate, and Advanced. The Performance Descriptors' statements offer a summary of what the learner at that range can do well. Learners in the Novice range of the Interpersonal Mode are good at engaging in conversations using memorized and practiced phrases and sentences, and forming questions using memorized and practiced patterns. To move to the Intermediate range, instructors need to provide support and practice of what learners in the Intermediate range can do well, namely taking on more of a responsibility to keep the conversation going and to accomplish the purpose behind the conversation (e.g., making plans, agreeing on a recommendation, finding out what they have in common).

Performance Descriptors: Interpersonal Mode

NOVICE RANGE
Expresses self in conversations on very familiar topics using a variety of words, phrases, simple sentences, and questions that have been highly practiced and memorized.

INTERMEDIATE RANGE
Expresses self and participates in conversations on familiar topics using sentences and series of sentences.
Handles short social interactions in everyday situations by asking and answering a variety of questions.
Can communicate about self, others, and everyday life.

ADVANCED RANGE
Expresses self fully to maintain conversations on familiar topics and new concrete social, academic, and work-related topics.
Can communicate in paragraph-length conversation about events with detail and organization.
Confidently handles situations with an unexpected complication.
Shares point of view in discussions.

The Sample Performance Indicators provide a bridge between the instructional setting and the real-world application of the language learned. The Global Statements point toward the curriculum-neutral Proficiency Guidelines but in terms of what can be developed, practiced, and assessed in a classroom. The Global Statements summarize what learners at that level can do independently, without the scaffolded support of the instructor. Rather than being seen as limiting the instructor's vision of what learners at a level "can do," the Global Statements need to be read as descriptive of the performance that will provide evidence of being at that level along the continuum of language performance, such as Novice High or Intermediate Low. The Sample Performance Indicators, like this Standards document, are intended to influence the design of curriculum and units of instruction, and describe the types of evidence to be collected through formative or summative assessments of performance. The Sample Indicators are examples of what an instructor will focus on for practice and assessment of the mode when targeting the Novice, Intermediate, Advanced, or even Superior ranges of performance. Like each Global Statement, the Sample Indicators at the same level show what the learner can do independently, with more specificity than in the Global Statement, helping the instructor identify what to work on to guide the learner to the next level. The Global Statements and the Sample Indicators point toward the communication strategies learners will need in order to move to higher levels of performance in the Interpersonal Mode, such as asking follow-up questions, asking for clarification and negotiating meaning, or expressing lack of understanding.

Sample Performance Indicators: Interpersonal Mode

GLOBAL STATEMENT	SAMPLE INDICATORS
NOVICE RANGE – INTERPERSONAL	
Novice Low Learners can communicate on some very familiar topics using single words and phrases that they have practiced and memorized.	**Novice Low Learners can** • greet peers • introduce self to someone • answer a few simple questions
Novice Mid Learners can communicate on very familiar topics using a variety of words and phrases that they have practiced and memorized.	**Novice Mid Learners can** • greet and leave people in a polite way • introduce self and others • answer a variety of simple questions • make some simple statements in a conversation • ask some simple questions • communicate basic information about self and people they know • communicate some basic information about their everyday lives
Novice High Learners can communicate and exchange information about familiar topics using phrases and simple sentences, sometimes supported by memorized language. They can usually handle short social interactions in everyday situations by asking and answering simple questions.	**Novice High Learners can** • exchange some personal information • exchange information using texts, graphs, or pictures • ask for and give simple directions • make plans with others • interact with others in everyday situations
INTERMEDIATE RANGE – INTERPERSONAL	
Intermediate Low Learners can participate in conversations on a number of familiar topics using simple sentences. They can handle short social interactions in everyday situations by asking and answering simple questions.	**Intermediate Low Learners can** • have a simple conversation on a number of everyday topics • ask and answer questions on factual information that is familiar to them • use the language to meet their basic needs in familiar situations
Intermediate Mid Learners can participate in conversations on familiar topics using sentences and series of sentences. They can handle short social interactions in everyday situations by asking and answering a variety of questions. They can usually say what they want to say about self and their everyday lives.	**Intermediate Mid Learners can** • start, maintain, and end a conversation on a variety of familiar topics • talk about their daily activities and personal preferences • use their language to handle tasks related to their personal needs • exchange information about subjects of special interest to them
Intermediate High Learners can participate with ease and confidence in conversations on familiar topics. They can usually talk about events and experiences in various time frames. They can usually describe people, places, and things. They can handle social interactions in everyday situations, sometimes even when there is an unexpected complication.	**Intermediate High Learners can** • exchange information related to areas of mutual interest • use their language to do a task that requires multiple steps • use their language to handle a situation that may have a complication

continued

GLOBAL STATEMENT	SAMPLE INDICATORS
ADVANCED RANGE – INTERPERSONAL	
Advanced Low Learners can participate in conversations about familiar topics that go beyond their everyday lives. They can talk in an organized way and with some detail about events and experiences in various time frames. They can describe people, places, and things in an organized way and with some detail. They can handle a familiar situation with an unexpected complication.	**Advanced Low Learners can** • participate in conversations on a wide variety of topics that go beyond their everyday lives • compare and contrast life in different locations and in different times • resolve an unexpected complication that arises in a familiar situation • conduct or participate in interviews
Advanced Mid Learners can express themselves fully not only on familiar topics but also on some concrete social, academic, and professional topics. They can talk in detail and in an organized way about events and experiences in various time frames. They can confidently handle routine situations with an unexpected complication. They can share their points of view in discussions on some complex issues.	**Advanced Mid Learners can** • communicate effectively on a wide variety of present, past, and future events • exchange general information on topics outside their fields of interest • handle a complication or unexpected turn of events
Advanced High Learners can express themselves freely and spontaneously, and for the most part accurately, on concrete topics and on most complex issues. They can usually support their opinion and develop hypotheses on topics of particular interest or personal expertise.	**Advanced High Learners can** • exchange complex information about academic and professional tasks • exchange detailed information on topics within and beyond their fields of interest • support their opinion and construct hypotheses
SUPERIOR RANGE – INTERPERSONAL	
Superior Learners can communicate with ease, accuracy, and fluency. They can participate fully and effectively in discussions on a variety of topics in formal and informal settings. They can discuss at length complex issues by structuring arguments and developing hypotheses.	**Superior Learners can** • support opinions clearly and precisely • discuss complex information in debates or meetings • participate with ease in complex discussions with multiple participants on a wide variety of topics

Sample Progress Indicators

These Sample Progress Indicators are examples of the variety of tasks that indicate how learners demonstrate language performance in the Novice, Intermediate, or Advanced range of the Interpersonal Mode of communication. The tasks provide a glimpse into what learners can do to develop, practice, and assess interpersonal communication. Rather than being organized by grade levels (as in previous editions of these National Standards), the Sample Progress Indicators are identified by performance range. Remember that learners at any age who are beginning to learn a new language start in the Novice range, even postsecondary and adult learners; learners in elementary grades may be in the Novice or Intermediate range, depending on the program model and their prior background experiences with the language. Notice how the other four goal areas (Cultures, Connections, Comparisons, and Communities) are embedded as the content (topic: What?) or context (situation: With whom, where, when?) for the Interpersonal task.

Interpersonal Communication

Interpretive Communication

Presentational Communication

Sample Progress Indicators, Novice Range

- Learners give and follow simple instructions in order to participate in age-appropriate classroom and/or cultural activities.
- Learners ask and answer questions about topics such as family, school events, and celebrations in person or via letters, email, voice chats, videochat, or instant messages.
- Learners share likes and dislikes with one another.
- Learners exchange descriptions of people and tangible products of the culture such as toys, clothing, types of dwellings, and foods with classmates.
- Learners exchange greetings, leave takings, and common classroom interactions using culturally appropriate gestures and oral expressions.

Sample Progress Indicators, Intermediate Range

- Learners follow and give directions for participating in age-appropriate cultural activities and investigating the function of products of the foreign culture. They ask and respond to questions for clarification.
- Learners exchange information about personal events, memorable experiences, and other school subjects with peers and/or members of the target cultures.
- Learners compare, contrast, and express opinions and preferences about the information gathered regarding events, experiences, and other school subjects.
- Learners acquire goods, services, or information orally and/or in writing.
- Learners develop and propose solutions to issues and problems related to the school or community through group work.

Sample Progress Indicators, Advanced Range

- Learners discuss, orally or in writing, current or past events that are of significance in the target culture or that are being studied in another subject.
- Learners develop and propose solutions to issues and problems that are of concern to members of their own and the target cultures through group work.
- Learners share their analyses and personal reactions to expository and literary texts with peers and/or speakers of the target language.
- Learners exchange, support, and discuss their opinions and individual perspectives with peers and/or speakers of the target language on a variety of topics dealing with contemporary and historical issues.

C INTERPRETIVE COMMUNICATION

Learners understand, interpret, and analyze what is heard, read, or viewed on a variety of topics.

This Standard focuses on the comprehension and interpretation of spoken, signed, and written language. Unlike the Interpersonal Communication Standard which combines a listener/speaker, reader/writer, or two people using ASL in two-way communication, the Interpretive Communication Standard involves one-way listening, reading, and viewing in which the learner engages with a variety of print and non-print materials, including multimedia, to appropriately interpret meanings that occur. Today visual literacy is added as a critical 21st century skill, defined as the learners' ability to "interpret, recognize, appreciate and understand information presented through visible actions, objects and symbols, natural or man-made." (Museums, Libraries, and 21st Century Skills, n.d.). Regardless of the type of material, various "layers" of interpretation exist, including literal interpretation, inferences, and cultural understanding. The interpretation of cultural meanings is a critical component of this Standard.

A key element that differentiates interpretive communication from the other two modes of communication is that the receiver does not have an immediate opportunity to negotiate meaning with the author or "presenter" or to ask for clarification; in essence, the reader, listener, or viewer must negotiate meaning with the document itself. For learners who come to language learning with no previous background in the language or associated culture(s), the context in which the language is experienced and the ability to control what they hear, read, and view may impact the development of comprehension. Depending on their level of interest and language ability, students who view a video online, for example, can play back part or all of the video several times for an increased level of understanding that is not available to them if that video is only provided to them for one viewing. Reading a narrative, newspaper article, or advertisement with visuals or engaging in prereading strategies at any level of language learning provides clues that help learners understand and analyze more readily than with print text alone. Learners may or may not be aware of the literacy strategies they commonly use in their native language and instructors should help learners focus on effective strategies to "make meaning" from what they hear, read, or view. In addition, content knowledge will often affect successful comprehension, for learners understand and interpret more easily materials that reflect their interests or for which they have some background. Heritage language learners, who have had exposure to the language and culture through their home life, frequently may be more advanced in their understanding of the spoken language than in their ability to read. For other learners, the ability to read at increased levels of proficiency may develop before the ability to comprehend rapidly spoken language. An exception to this assumption may be made for learners of languages with non-Roman writing systems, for whom reading proficiency at any level may develop more slowly. As opposed to language that is directly heard or viewed, the reading aspects of this Standard make it particularly relevant to the learning of classical languages.

Learner success in interpreting a document (written or audio/video) is based upon a complex combination of the content and context of the message, the learner's own background knowledge, the motivation or interest to understand, control over effective interpretive strategies, and the instructional task as defined by the teacher. An additional confounding factor is that the reading, listening, or viewing is not directly observable; it takes place in the learner's mind as meaning is constructed. In the Interpersonal Mode, the student expression can be heard, viewed, negotiated, or corrected; in the Presentational Mode, the spoken, written, or media presentation is equally visible to the audience for which it has been designed. For the Interpretive Mode, a way to demonstrate the degree of meaning-making must be designed that does not rely upon the level of speech in the target language. For beginning learners, their proficiency in answering falls short of how much they actually understand from a document; they often acquire much more information than they can express in the target language. Furthermore, this constellation of factors means that a given document cannot be neatly pegged for students at a given proficiency range so the designations of Novice, Intermediate, and Advanced have to be flexible. For example, students who may be Intermediate learners in most tasks may move well beyond that when reading an article or viewing a video clip on a topic with which they are highly knowledgeable and motivated to interpret. A story might be interpreted by Novices and Intermediates for plot and characters and by Advanced learners for deeper meanings and literary purposes. Age also plays a role just as *Alice in Wonderland* or *Le Petit Prince* hold different messages for the child, young adult, and adult reader. There is no hierarchy of texts or topics or genres associated with a given reader/listener/ viewer; there is no firm sequence of how students get the meaning of a passage. In some cases, learners may understand a main idea—and as they reread and rewatch, they may pick up supporting details. But in other cases, they may quickly pick up on a few of the details and during the next reading/watching see the main ideas emerge. Interpretation is not linear; it is an iterative process as learners go back and forth to assemble the puzzle of meaningfulness.

The choice of documents, their content, and their alignment with a theme being pursued, is made in consideration of learners' background knowledge and interests. The genre of the documents also provides students with expectations that further comprehension just as happens in first language literacy. It surprises some that research has shown that longer passages have benefits over very short ones. A narrative with a story line allows for the learner to follow a plot line, assemble character traits and expectations, build anticipation of episodes and confirm or reject hypotheses, take advantage of repetition and redundancies; these are the kinds of texts enjoyed by young children as they move from listening and following a story to reading it. Stories or informational texts exploit length to reword and to develop ideas that very short tight texts do not; the latter tend to reduce redundancy and require greater background from the reader/listener/viewer to fill in the spaces making the seemingly simple less so. In the classroom, the educator facilitates the interpretive process until learners can move to independent and extensive reading/listening/viewing. A headline is just words and barely a phrase, but that makes it harder to understand and easier to miscue than does a paragraph.

Authentic materials generally abide by certain frameworks associated with the genre, and these can assist greatly in comprehension. Students bring expectations of genre from their first language to apply to the new language with adaptations to cultural differences as needed. A biographical piece, whether a social networking profile, a wiki chart, or a chapter or book, entails certain expectations in the coverage of information. A graphic organizer might be a device for students to chart what they understand—and reading about a person whose story is compelling and whose name or work is familiar influences comprehension. Interviews have a question-and-answer framework so that readers/listeners/viewers use the interaction to their benefit: Understanding the question helps the learner frame the response, just as when the learner is not sure of the question the response may help with understanding the original question. Fables and legends tend to include a moral or lesson as they reveal characteristics valued by a culture. News articles illustrate the journalistic details of who, when, where, what, and how. Teachers can help learners become skillful at accessing the structure of the text and its purpose in order to improve their comprehension.

Unique Nature of Performance in the Interpretive Mode

Second language learners use a variety of strategies acquired in their first language to construct meaning in the second language. Improving performance in the Interpretive Mode is not just about accessing more complex texts, rather it is through consciously using a wider variety of strategies to understand what is heard, read, or viewed, including top-down strategies (using background knowledge and context clues to figure out the meaning) as well as bottom-up strategies (discriminating between sounds and letters or recognizing characters, recognizing word-order patterns, analyzing sentence structure, examining parts of words to try to decipher meaning). In learners' first language, phonics or character recognition work because they have a bank of oral language that they can convert to written. In learners' second language, educators need to first activate top-down strategies so learners understand the overall meaning and context before using bottom-up strategies to refine their initial understanding. Depending on their familiarity with the topic, genre, or vocabulary, learners may demonstrate comprehension as a reader, listener, or viewer beyond the level they demonstrate in the productive modes of Interpersonal and Presentational Communication. Therefore, for the Interpretive Mode, the charts of the Performance Descriptors and Sample Performance Indicators (Can-Do Statements) are not included here as they are for the Interpersonal and Presentational Modes. For reference, the Appendix provides the Performance Descriptors for the Interpretive Mode and Can-Do Statements for Listening and Reading.

Sample Progress Indicators

These Sample Progress Indicators are examples of the variety of tasks that indicate how learners demonstrate language performance in the Novice, Intermediate, or Advanced range of the Interpretive Mode of communication. The tasks provide a glimpse into what learners can do to develop, practice, and assess interpretive communication. Rather than being organized by grade levels (as in previous editions of these National Standards), the Sample Progress Indicators are now identified by performance range. Remember that learners at any age who are beginning to learn a new language start in the Novice range, even postsecondary and adult learners; learners in elementary grades may be in the Novice or Intermediate range, depending on the program model and their prior background experiences with the language. Notice how the other four goal areas (Cultures, Connections, Comparisons, and Communities) are embedded as the content (topic: What?) or context (situation: With whom, where, when?) for the Interpretive task.

Sample Progress Indicators, Novice Range

- Learners list key actions from developmentally appropriate narratives such as personal anecdotes, familiar fairy tales, and narratives based on familiar themes.
- Learners identify people and objects in their environment or from other school subjects, based on oral and written descriptions.

- Learners report out the content of brief, written messages and short personal notes on familiar topics such as family, school events, and celebrations.
- Learners identify the principal characters of stories or children's literature and dramatize the main themes and ideas.
- Learners identify the principal message contained in various media such as illustrated texts, posters, or advertisements.
- Learners interpret the meaning of gestures, intonation, and other visual or auditory cues.

Sample Progress Indicators, Intermediate Range

- Learners restate information from short articles and postings related to other school subjects.
- Learners react to messages in video clips from the target culture on current issues of interest to peers.
- Learners locate key information from announcements and messages connected to daily activities in the target culture.
- Learners relate the main themes and significant details on topics from other subjects and products of the cultures as presented on TV, radio, video, or live presentations.
- Learners describe the main themes and significant details on topics from other subjects and products of the cultures as found in newspapers, magazines, websites, or other printed sources for target language audiences.
- Learners identify the principal characters and discuss the main ideas and themes in selected literary texts.
- Learners use knowledge acquired in other settings and from other subject areas to comprehend spoken and written messages in the target languages.

Sample Progress Indicators, Advanced Range

- Learners discuss the main ideas and significant details of live and recorded discussions, lectures, and presentations on current or past events from the target culture or that are being studied in another class.
- Learners summarize the principal elements of non-fiction articles in newspapers, magazines, and websites on topics of current and historical importance to members of the culture.
- Learners analyze the main plot, subplot, characters, their descriptions, roles, and significance in authentic literary texts.
- Learners compare and contrast cultural nuances of meaning in written and spoken language as expressed by speakers of the target language in formal and informal settings.
- Learners describe cultural nuances of meaning in expressive products of the culture, including selections from various literary genres and the visual arts.

C PRESENTATIONAL COMMUNICATION

Learners present information, concepts, and ideas to inform, explain, persuade, and narrate on a variety of topics using appropriate media and adapting to various audiences of listeners, readers, or viewers.

This Standard is concerned with the creation of a message through spoken, signed, or written communication that is one way—in that interaction with the speaker, signer, writer, or media producer is not part of the presentational task. Presentational communication results in a product that may be polished, edited, or rehearsed (e.g., multimedia presentation, dramatization, article) or may be "on demand" without the opportunity for polishing or expectation of editing (e.g., journal entry, debate rebuttal, announcement). The presentational performance should be designed for a targeted audience of one or more, real or simulated. Consequently, the learner needs to incorporate into his/her message a comprehensible level of language accuracy and a style appropriate to expectations of the audience and the presentational format (e.g., poster, original skit, digital brochure, TV ad, electronic infobrief, video podcast, graph of data, letter to the editor, short film, poem or short story). During the presentational task, the learner is not interacting with the audience in the Interpersonal Mode; however, following the presentational task, the learner might engage in an interpersonal (two-way) discussion with the audience. Unlike interpersonal communication where individuals negotiate meaning in a spontaneous setting, presentational tasks generally require a process of generating ideas, drafting, using feedback to revise, and producing a final product. Through interpretive tasks, learners build up their presentational skills, working with materials—including various media—that provide models for acquiring authentic linguistic and cultural patterns and the use of styles suitable for different presentational products.

Heritage language learners often may write in ways that closely resemble the spoken language. Moreover, they may have good control over informal oral styles that may not be the most appropriate choice in presentational formats. These learners need to develop their ability to write and speak using a variety of styles adjusted to match the requirements of the presentational communication and the intended audience.

Nonnative learners in the second language classroom bring prior literacy to presentational tasks and may early on stretch beyond the Novice level because they are already accustomed to presenting ideas in the form of sentences in their first language. Unless the task requires mere labeling, they work to express meaning with fuller expression, thinking in sentences and trying to create them. They make frequent mistakes in accuracy using their new language, but the issue of accuracy can be addressed through the nature of the presentational task, with the instructor coaching the drafting, revising, and final "publishing" of the task.

The Continuum of Language Performance in the Presentational Mode

To guide curriculum, instruction, and assessment, this document connects the Communication Standards with two useful descriptions of language performance: the Performance Descriptors for Language Learners (ACTFL, 2012a) and the NCSSFL-ACTFL Can-Do Statements (2013).

The Performance Descriptors describe the range of performance that is the result of instruction in an instructional setting. The performance is described for three levels: Novice, Intermediate, and Advanced. The Performance Descriptors' statements offer a summary of where to focus the instructor's coaching. Learners in the Novice range of the Presentational Mode need to practice expressing their own thoughts in order to move into the Intermediate range. Learners in the Intermediate range of the Presentational Mode need to practice creating cohesive paragraphs, such as telling a story.

Performance Descriptors: Presentational Mode

NOVICE RANGE
Communicates information on very familiar topics using a variety of words, phrases, and sentences that have been practiced and memorized.
INTERMEDIATE RANGE
Communicates information and expresses own thoughts about familiar topics using sentences and series of sentences.
ADVANCED RANGE
Communicates information and expresses self with detail and organization on familiar and some new concrete topics using paragraphs.

The Sample Performance Indicators provide a bridge between the instructional setting (language performance) and the real-world application of the language learned (proficiency). The Global Statements summarize what learners at that level can do independently, without the scaffolded support of the instructor. The Sample Indicators at the same level show what the learner can do with more specificity than in each Global Statement; the Sample Indicators are descriptive of the variety of performances that will provide evidence of being at that level along the continuum of language performance.

Sample Performance Indicators: Presentational Mode – Speaking

GLOBAL STATEMENT	SAMPLE INDICATORS
NOVICE RANGE – PRESENTATIONAL SPEAKING	
Novice Low Learners can present information about themselves and some other very familiar topics using single words or memorized phrases.	**Novice Low Learners can** • recite words and phrases that they have learned • state the names of familiar people, places, and objects in pictures and posters using words or memorized phrases • introduce self to a group • recite short memorized phrases, parts of poems, and rhymes

continued

GLOBAL STATEMENT	SAMPLE INDICATORS
Novice Mid Learners can present information about themselves and some other very familiar topics using a variety of words, phrases, and memorized expressions.	**Novice Mid Learners can** • present information about self and others using words and phrases • express their likes and dislikes using words, phrases, and memorized expressions • present information about familiar items in their immediate environment • talk about their daily activities using words, phrases, and memorized expressions • present simple information about something they learned using words, phrases, and memorized expressions
Novice High Learners can present basic information on familiar topics using language they have practiced using phrases and simple sentences.	**Novice High Learners can** • present information about their lives using phrases and simple sentences • tell about a familiar experience or event using phrases and simple sentences • present basic information about a familiar person, place, or thing using phrases and simple sentences • present information about others using phrases and simple sentences • give basic instructions on how to make or do something using phrases and simple sentences • present basic information about things they have learned using phrases and simple sentences
INTERMEDIATE RANGE – PRESENTATIONAL SPEAKING	
Intermediate Low Learners can present information on most familiar topics using a series of simple sentences.	**Intermediate Low Learners can** • talk about people, activities, events, and experiences • express their needs and wants • present information on plans, instructions, and directions • present songs, short skits, or dramatic readings • express their preferences on topics of interest
Intermediate Mid Learners can make presentations on a wide variety of familiar topics using connected sentences.	**Intermediate Mid Learners can** • make a presentation about their personal and social experiences • make a presentation on something they have learned or researched • make a presentation about common interests and issues and state their viewpoint
Intermediate High Learners can make presentations in a generally organized way on school, work, and community topics, and on topics they have researched. They can make presentations on some events and experiences in various time frames.	**Intermediate High Learners can** • present information on academic and work topics • make a presentation on events, activities, and topics of particular interest • present their points of view and provide reasons to support them

continued

Interpersonal Communication

Interpretive Communication

Presentational Communication

GLOBAL STATEMENT	SAMPLE INDICATORS
ADVANCED RANGE – PRESENTATIONAL SPEAKING	
Advanced Low Learners can deliver organized presentations appropriate to their audience on a variety of topics. They can present information about events and experiences in various time frames.	**Advanced Low Learners can** • deliver short presentations on a number of academic and workplace topics • deliver short presentations on social and cultural topics • explain issues of public and community interest, including different viewpoints • deliver presentations for a specific audience
Advanced Mid Learners can deliver well-organized presentations on concrete social, academic, and professional topics. They can present detailed information about events and experiences in various time frames.	**Advanced Mid Learners can** • present information about events of public or personal interest • convey their ideas and elaborate on a variety of academic topics • give presentations with ease and detail on a wide variety of topics related to professional interests
Advanced High Learners can deliver detailed presentations, usually with accuracy, clarity, and precision, on a variety of topics and issues related to community interests and some special fields of expertise.	**Advanced High Learners can** • present complex information on many concrete topics and related issues • present a viewpoint with supporting arguments on a complex issue • use appropriate presentational conventions and strategies
SUPERIOR RANGE – PRESENTATIONAL SPEAKING	
Superior Learners can deliver detailed presentations with accuracy, clarity, and precision to a wide variety of audiences on topics and issues ranging from broad general interests to areas of specialized expertise.	**Superior Learners can** • give a clearly articulated and well-structured presentation on a complex topic or issue • adapt the language in a presentation for casual, professional, or general public audiences • depart from the prepared text of a presentation when appropriate

Sample Performance Indicators: Presentational Mode – Writing

GLOBAL STATEMENT	SAMPLE INDICATORS
NOVICE RANGE – PRESENTATIONAL WRITING	
Novice Low Learners can copy some familiar words, characters, or phrases.	**Novice Low Learners can** • copy some characters or letters and words that they see on the wall or board, in a book, or on the computer • write words and phrases that they have learned • label familiar people, places, and objects in pictures and posters

continued

GLOBAL STATEMENT	SAMPLE INDICATORS
Novice Mid Learners can write lists and memorized phrases on familiar topics.	**Novice Mid Learners can** • fill out a simple form with some basic personal information • write about themselves using learned phrases and memorized expressions • list their daily activities and write lists that help them in their day-to-day lives • write notes about something they have learned using lists, phrases, and memorized expressions
Novice High Learners can write short messages and notes on familiar topics related to everyday life.	**Novice High Learners can** • write information about their daily life in a letter, blog, discussion board, or email message • write short notes using phrases and simple sentences • write about a familiar experience or event using practiced material • write basic information about things they have learned • ask for information in writing
INTERMEDIATE RANGE – PRESENTATIONAL WRITING	
Intermediate Low Learners can write briefly about most familiar topics and present information using a series of simple sentences.	**Intermediate Low Learners can** • write about people, activities, events, and experiences • prepare materials for a presentation • write about topics of interest • write basic instructions on how to make or do something • write questions to obtain information
Intermediate Mid Learners can write on a wide variety of familiar topics using connected sentences.	**Intermediate Mid Learners can** • write messages and announcements • write short reports about something they have learned or researched • compose communications for public distribution
Intermediate High Learners can write on topics related to school, work, and community in a generally organized way. They can write some simple paragraphs about events and experiences in various time frames.	**Intermediate High Learners can** • write about school and academic topics • write about work and career topics • write about community topics and events • write about entertainment or a social event
ADVANCED RANGE – PRESENTATIONAL WRITING	
Advanced Low Learners can write on general interest, academic, and professional topics. They can write organized paragraphs about events and experiences in various time frames.	**Advanced Low Learners can** • meet basic school and academic writing needs • meet basic work and career writing needs • meet basic social and civic writing needs

continued

Interpersonal Communication

Interpretive Communication

Presentational Communication

GLOBAL STATEMENT	SAMPLE INDICATORS
Advanced Mid Learners can write on a wide variety of general interest, professional, and academic topics. They can write well-organized, detailed paragraphs in various time frames.	**Advanced Mid Learners can** • write well-organized texts for a variety of academic purposes • write well-organized texts for a variety of professional purposes • write well-organized texts for a variety of general interest purposes
Advanced High Learners can write extensively with significant precision and detail on a variety of topics, most complex issues, and some special fields of expertise.	**Advanced High Learners can** • write using target language and culture conventions to present and elaborate a point of view • write using target language and culture conventions for informal purposes • write using target language and culture conventions for formal purposes
SUPERIOR RANGE – PRESENTATIONAL WRITING	
Superior Learners can write about complex and abstract issues ranging from topics of broad general interests to areas of specialized expertise using standard structure, lexicon, and writing protocols.	**Superior Learners can** • write effectively about complex and abstract issues of general interest • write about complex and abstract issues on academic and professional topics • develop an argument using the writing mechanics and organizational style of the target language and culture

Sample Progress Indicators

These Sample Progress Indicators are examples of the variety of tasks that indicate how learners demonstrate language performance in the Novice, Intermediate, or Advanced range of the Presentational Mode of communication. The tasks provide a glimpse into what learners can do to develop, practice, and assess presentational communication. Rather than being organized by grade levels (as in previous editions of these National Standards), the Sample Progress Indicators are identified by performance range. Learners at any age who are beginning to learn a new language start in the Novice range, even postsecondary and adult learners; learners in elementary grades may be in the Novice or Intermediate range, depending on the program model and their prior background experiences with the language. Notice how the other four goal areas (Cultures, Connections, Comparisons, and Communities) are embedded as the content (topic: What?) or context (situation: With whom, where, when?) for the Presentational task.

Sample Progress Indicators, Novice Range

- Learners prepare illustrated stories about activities or events in their environment and share these stories and events with an audience in the school or community or post them to a website.
- Learners dramatize and video songs, short anecdotes, or poetry commonly known by peers in the target culture and post them to the school website or to a video sharing website.

- Learners record short oral notes and messages, or write reports, about people and things in their school environment and post the information for a partner language class either locally or abroad.
- Learners create a poster for Do's and Don'ts for Earth Day.
- Learners draw or produce a video ad about products and/or practices of their own culture to peers in the target culture.

Sample Progress Indicators, Intermediate Range

- Learners dramatize short plays, original skits, recite selected poems and anecdotes, and perform songs in the language for a school-related event such as a board meeting or PTA meeting or campus festival.
- Learners prepare video recorded messages to share locally or with school peers and/or members of the target cultures on topics of personal interest.
- Learners create a brochure that highlights things to see and do in their community for visitors from the target culture.
- Learners prepare stories or brief written reports about personal experiences, events, or other school subjects to share with classmates and/or members of the target cultures.
- Learners create and narrate a PowerPoint presentation on a current global concern.
- Learners prepare an oral or written summary of the plot and characters in selected pieces of age-appropriate literature.

Sample Progress Indicators, Advanced Range

- Learners write a news article or critique on a topic from another discipline such as world history, geography, the arts, or mathematics.
- Learners perform scenes from a play and/or recite poems or excerpts from short stories commonly read by speakers of the target language.
- Learners create stories and poems, short plays, or skits based on personal experiences and exposure to themes, ideas, and perspectives from the target culture.
- Learners design a written or video production that analyzes expressive products of the culture, from literary genres or the fine arts.
- Learners summarize the content of an article or documentary intended for native speakers for a school or local publication or blog.
- Learners write a letter or an article describing and analyzing an issue for a student publication.
- Learners prepare a research-based analysis of a current event from the perspective of both the United States and target cultures.

GOAL AREA: CULTURES

Interact with cultural competence and understanding

RATIONALE

The study of other cultures is deeply intertwined with the study of other languages. We learn to understand another culture and interact appropriately within it through the learning of its language for purposes of communication in the Interpersonal, Interpretive, and Presentational Modes. The inherent connections between the culture that is lived and the language that is expressed can only be realized by those who possess knowledge and understanding of both. Learning about and experiencing another culture in both simulated and authentic situations, either real or virtual, enable students to understand that particular culture on its own terms. Developing an understanding and awareness of other cultures' perspectives is critical in the development of global competence, an essential theme in preparing learners for life and work in the 21st century. All students need to understand diverse cultural perspectives that exist both within the United States and other countries in order to function appropriately in varied cultural and linguistic contexts that they may encounter in their future. It is fundamental to develop an awareness of other people's world views and the rituals and patterns of behavior that characterize their world, as well as the products that the culture has created and the reasons for their existence. Additionally, learners in the 21st century must recognize the contributions of other cultures to the world at large and the possible solutions that they may offer to common challenges and problems faced in other parts of our globe.

DISCUSSION

What Is Culture? The term "culture" is generally understood to include the philosophical perspectives, the behavioral practices, and the products—both tangible and intangible—of a society. The diagram on the next page illustrates how the products and practices are derived from the perspectives that form the world view of a cultural group. It also shows how these three components of culture are closely interrelated.

Many models for the study of culture exist; the Framework presented here incorporates elements of a number of them. The interplay of products, practices, and perspectives acts as an organizer that is adaptable for learners of all ages, for educators at all levels, and for developers of educational materials. The model should also be considered as a dynamic one. Especially in today's rapidly changing world of the 21st century with its wealth of ever-increasing technological tools, culture undergoes changes in communities and countries across the globe. Depending on populations and localities around the world, what was viewed as traditional even a few decades ago may no longer be so in today's global society, or it may be restricted to certain areas or cultural groups within a country but cannot be generalized to a total population. Consequently, culture cannot be understood as being static in terms of its products, practices and underlying perspectives but rather we must remain open to new hypotheses and questions as we seek to interact with cultural competence and understanding in the world of today and of the future.

CULTURES FRAMEWORK

PERSPECTIVES
(Meanings, attitudes, values, ideas)

PRACTICES
(Patterns of social interactions)

PRODUCTS
(Books, tools, foods, laws, music, games)

Because language is the primary vehicle for expressing cultural perspectives and participating in social practices, the study of a language provides multiple opportunities for learners to investigate the relationships between the perspectives and the practices and products of a particular culture, as well as to develop insights about a culture that are available in no other way. In reality, the true content of a language course or program is not discrete elements of grammar and vocabulary, but rather the cultures expressed through the language. Neither students nor their teachers can know every product, practice, or related perspective about the target cultures and the dynamic changes that occur as one is learning. What is important, however, is that they become skilled observers and interpreters of other cultures and that they maintain insights and hypotheses as they reflect upon their current knowledge and skills while also acquiring new information and experiences.

A significant shift in how culture is taught in the language classroom is the move away from teaching isolated facts to integrating culture with language. Traditionally, culture appeared as notes on the page of a textbook, and the learner was more of a passive observer, like a traveler who only looks at another culture through the lens of his or her own. At the heart of the World-Readiness Standards for Learning Languages is the attitude of being an explorer, using language to investigate, explain, and reflect on how perspectives are exhibited in the practices and products of a culture. Through language learning experiences, learners increase their background knowledge of the cultures that speak the language being studied and also develop the skills of observing and researching questions that surface around cultural perspectives, practices, and products.

Avoiding Cultural Misunderstandings. People who share the same native language share many common perspectives, practices, and products. Speakers of a single language may live in parts of the world divided by great distances. Despite ever-increasing technology that can link individual speakers and communities virtually anywhere and anytime, the speakers of a single language may belong to different cultures. Even though they share a language, factors such as time, geographical location, and various profound and unique experiences cause groups to differ from one another with different traditions and expressions. To apply a single set of criteria when teaching, learning, and interacting with those cultures would be to ignore the current reality and fail to respect the practices, products, and underlying perspectives of disparate cultural groups. To assume, for example, that the Spanish-speaking cultures in Latin America are essentially the same as the cultures of Spain, or the cultures of immigrants from Mexico or the Caribbean living in the United States, is to deny the special identity of each group. Without awareness of these profound differences, learners' ensuing impressions and interactions may result in misunderstandings and the inability to communicate appropriately. The same can be said for the Arabic-speaking cultures of Africa and the Middle East, as well as with the numerous Arabic-speaking immigrant groups in the United States originally from Syria, Egypt, or Iraq. Such examples of cultural diversity within commonly shared languages are numerous and significant. Clearly, cultural diversity is found within a single country, as in the pluralistic and ever-changing society of the United States.

Learners must be able to recognize that members of one culture tend to make assumptions and draw corresponding conclusions about other cultures based upon their own values, and at the same time should understand that such conclusions are not accurate or reliable. Opinions and attitudes, both hidden and expressed, are often based upon a superficial examination of other cultures using criteria that can be applied with validity only to one's own culture. The erroneous judgments that result from such assumptions, born of a lack of adequate information, understanding, and sensitivity, eventually lead to negative reactions to members of different cultures. To counteract this tendency, educators must provide learning activities appropriate to the learners' level and language ability that explore the process of stereotyping and the role that stereotypes play in forming and sustaining prejudice. Finally, it is critical to provide opportunities for many different kinds of interaction, both real and virtual, with members of other cultures so that learners draw informed conclusions; develop sensitivity to the perspectives, practices, and products of others; and gain confidence in interacting appropriately. Learners in the United States need a nuanced understanding of the nation's multiple and shifting cultural identifies when making comparisons to cultures abroad. Learners often draw conclusions based on simplistic or unexamined views of their own culture. Educators can help learners think critically and look out for their blind spots in understanding their own culture as they seek to understand other cultures.

Instructional Approaches. In the survey of how teachers were implementing the National Standards for Learning Languages (Phillips & Abbott, 2011) a number of teachers expressed their own hesitancy in teaching toward the Cultures Standards due to personal lack of experience in a target language country or just limited experience (e.g., familiar with Mexico but not Spain). The Cultural Framework that illustrates the relationship among products, practices, and perspectives can serve to organize teachers' continued growth in this area even as they use it with students. Interpretive language tasks with authentic materials and interpersonal communication with native speakers, either in a real or virtual environment, can routinely include a focus on drawing out information about products and practices; further evidence and research can bring forth insights into the perspectives—that is, the values, attitudes represented now or in the past, and their relationship to cultural products and practices. In terms of instructional approaches, when one leads with culture, language will follow. Rather than adding culture as an afterthought, beginning a new unit of instruction by examining cultural images and artifacts and authentic materials, can tap learners' interests. As learners start asking questions about cultural products and practices, educators can provide the language they need to explore those questions. Through the motivation of exploring culture, learners acquire the language the need. This is the opposite of starting with vocabulary or structures and searching for motivating content to get learners to use that language. Teachers might also want to explore some of the models for intercultural competence to help them identify concepts included in perspectives (or cultural universals in some models), seeking out what is shared across cultures. These include family or gender roles, religious beliefs, individual versus community responsibilities, the relationship of man versus nature, and the like. These overarching categories encompass a multitude of related products and practices.

Teaching Similarities and Differences. While no one doubts that both similarities and differences exist among any given cultures, a question that concerns many teachers is which to present first. There is some evidence to show that a positive point of departure—underscoring ways in which members of the other culture share similar interests, behaviors, and belief systems with language learners in the United States—establishes a favorable mindset toward speakers of the other language and an easier entry into understanding the culture and its language. It is essential, however, that cultural differences not be swept under a pedagogical rug. It is the differences in world view and the behavior patterns based on those differing assumptions and values that often give rise to misunderstandings and conflict. It is important to help learners expect differences and learn how to explain and analyze observed differences and their relationship to one or more cultural perspectives (i.e., how to put differences into perspective within the cultural framework of the other language). At every stage of language learning, both similarities and differences among the students' own culture and the other cultures should be included in instructional opportunities. When learners overlook similarities and shared universal values, they risk developing a bias of only seeing differences and being blind to similarities of cultures. Interactions with representatives of the other cultures and experience with a variety of cultural expressions (e.g., personal anecdotes, poetry, headlines, editorials, laws, music, museums, trains, pets) help learners shape their own awarenesses and increase their abilities to function appropriately in diverse cultural and linguistic contexts. This personal exploration in the language of the culture enables learners to develop cross-cultural understanding and respect while also helping them reflect on their own culture in ways they may not have considered previously.

The Specific Role of Language Learning. One of the most enduring aspects of learning cultural knowledge and skills is the learner's actual participation in the exchange of information and ideas among members of various cultures using the language. While a great deal of information about other cultures can be gained through the study of other disciplines, such as the social sciences and the arts, only the study of a world language empowers learners to engage successfully in meaningful interaction, both orally and in writing, with members of other cultures and the multitude of materials and media that they produce. In our society of the 21st century, language learning and cultural competence are key components not only to understanding and addressing global issues but also to living and working successfully within both the ever-increasing multicultural composition of the United States as well as the many cultures and subcultures existing outside our borders. The perspectives, practices, and products of culture—be they historical or contemporary—can be shared through investigation, explanation, and reflection in real or virtual environments with members of the culture in which they originated. This new "insider's" perspective, only available through the study of another language, is the true catalyst for cross-cultural understanding.

The development of interculturality (already described under the C of Communication) is also enhanced through acquisition of another language. The National Council of State Supervisors for Languages (NCSSFL) describes interculturality in connection with the LinguaFolio through which learners reflect on their growth in using language and understanding cultures. Interculturality refers to "the interaction of people from different cultural backgrounds, using authentic language appropriately to demonstrate knowledge and understanding of the cultures. . . . Intercultural experiences provide the most meaningful opportunities for developing capacity in a language." (NCSSFL, 2010). Language allows for that interaction and for a deeper experience of another culture leading to an evaluation of one's perceptions and reactions. Language frames the way people view themselves and others.

Cultures Standards

STANDARDS

 Relating Cultural Practices to Perspectives

 Relating Cultural Products to Perspectives

The Cultures goal includes two Standards. They emphasize the practices and the products of cultures, both in relationship to cultural perspectives. Without a focus on the underlying perspectives, learners may be tempted to view certain practices or products as isolated or strange elements of a particular culture and thereby acquire the stereotypes that their language study should be precluding. The rationale for these Standards is to "interact with cultural competence and understanding." This underscores the link of languages with cultures.

C RELATING CULTURAL PRACTICES TO PERSPECTIVES

Learners use the language to investigate, explain, and reflect on the relationship between the practices and perspectives of the cultures studied.

This Standard focuses on the practices that are derived from the traditional ideas, attitudes, and values (i.e., perspectives) of a culture. "Cultural practices" refer to patterns of behavior accepted by a society and comprise aspects of culture such as greetings, when meals are served, at what age children start school, how people spend their weekends, rites of passage, the use of forms of discourse, the social "pecking order," and the use of space. In short, they represent the knowledge of "what to do when and where." It is important to understand and be able to explain the relationship between these practices and the underlying perspectives that represent the culture's view of the world, with the learner's ultimate goal being to function appropriately in diverse contexts.

For example, in some Asian cultures, members are positioned (a perspective) on a hierarchical scale based on age, social status, education, or similar variables. In those cultures, the exchange of business cards (a product) that provide key information is a helpful practice. Because these cards facilitate social interaction and are treated with respect in those cultures, one should not simply place the business card hastily into one's pocket or scribble another name or telephone number on the card (offensive practices). The information on the card also directly affects the nonverbal behavior (practice) of those involved in the communicative interaction, as well as the choice of linguistic forms (products) that indicate status.

In France, cuisine is more highly valued (a perspective) when prepared with fresh, seasonal, and local ingredients (products), using specific methods and tools (practices). Because meals are considered important events (a perspective), one should not interrupt a meal, even a business lunch, for external communications or transactions (inappropriate practices). During the meal, certain topics of conversation, especially food and drink, are preferred, while others, such as money and work, are generally to be avoided.

At all levels of language learning, learners could consider using either the triangle in the Cultures Framework or advanced organizers (e.g., Venn diagram, chart, journal, word cloud generator) to record observations, reflections, and open questions as they use the language to increase their cultural understanding and competence.

Sample Progress Indicators

Following are examples of learners using language to investigate, explain, and reflect on the three Ps of Culture (practices, products, and perspectives). These are divided into additional examples from the Novice, Intermediate, and Advanced ranges to reflect the language level the learner uses, not to signal a higher degree of cultural understanding. There is no guarantee that because learners are able to use language in the Advanced range that they have internalized culturally appropriate greetings, such as saying "Bonjour, Madame" upon entering a shop in France. Even though the learner knows how to say it and has learned that it is the right thing to say, it may not yet be an automatic reaction. Learners at any age may be beginners in a new language and in the Novice range of language performance. The Sample Progress Indicators for learners at the Intermediate level describe potential performance of elementary learners in programs with sufficient time to reach that level of language performance and include elementary learners in immersion or dual language programs, plus secondary and postsecondary learners with more years of learning. The Sample Progress Indicators for learners at the Advanced level describe potential performance of secondary learners from immersion or dual language programs or strong elementary programs, secondary native or heritage speakers of the language, and postsecondary learners with sufficient years of learning.

Sample Progress Indicators

NOVICE RANGE LEARNERS

To interact with cultural competence and understanding

Novice Learners

- Learners use appropriate gestures and oral expressions for greetings, leave takings, and common classroom or social interactions (e.g., please, thank you, may I . . .).
- Learners participate in or simulate age-appropriate cultural activities such as games, birthday celebrations, storytelling, and dramatizations.
- Learners create or propose simple cultural triangles connecting practices to associated products and perspectives.

Novice Learners in Elementary School

- Learners in Grades K–5 observe and imitate simple patterns of behavior at school (e.g., standing when teacher enters room, greeting teacher at start of class).
- Learners in Grades K–5 use words and phrases to describe what people from the target culture are doing in photos and short video clips and ask simple questions about characteristics of daily life after looking at the photos or short videos.
- Learners in Grades 3–5 list practices observed in a video of a festival or holiday celebrated in the target culture.

Novice Learners in Middle School and High School

- Learners use appropriate gestures in classroom interactions (e.g., standing when an adult enters the room or when responding to a question, using fingers to count, raising hand to respond to a question).
- Learners imitate appropriate etiquette from the target culture at mealtime.
- Learners list practices observed in a video of a practice from the target culture.
- Learners role play simple interactions in stores and restaurants in the target culture.

Novice Learners at the Postsecondary Level

- Learners observe, identify, and/or imitate simple patterns of behavior or interaction in various settings such as campus, family, and the community.
- Learners list and identify practices observed in a video (e.g., of an event or celebration) that are outcomes of perspectives of the target culture.

Sample Progress Indicators

INTERMEDIATE RANGE LEARNERS

To interact with cultural competence and understanding

Intermediate Learners

- Learners observe, analyze, and exchange information on patterns of behavior typical of their peer group in the culture, such as observing and analyzing how different ways of greeting and leave-taking reflect the relationships between people in the target culture.
- Learners participate in age-appropriate cultural practices such as games (e.g., role of leader, taking turns), sports, and entertainment (e.g., music, dance, drama).

Intermediate Learners in Elementary School

- Learners in Grades 3–5 distinguish informal and formal ways to address classmates and adults (e.g., teachers or principal).
- Learners in Grades 3–5 role play simple situations from the target culture such as buying a snack (e.g., ice cream cone, soda) using culturally appropriate gestures and language.
- Learners in Grades 3–5 use some culturally appropriate gestures and expressions in their interactions with others.
- Learners in Grades 3–5 create cultural triangles connecting practices to associated products and perspectives, beginning to analyze the relationship among the practices, products, and perspectives.

Intermediate Learners in Middle School and High School

- Learners identify and analyze cultural practices from authentic materials such as videos and news articles.
- Learners engage in conversations with native speakers demonstrating an awareness of how to be culturally respectful.
- Learners use formal and informal forms of address appropriately in rehearsed situations.
- Learners role play culturally appropriate interactions with shopkeepers, ticket sellers, waiters, bus and taxi drivers, etc. in the target culture.
- Learners begin to adjust language and message to acknowledge audiences with different cultural backgrounds.
- Learners suggest cultural triangles with reasons connecting practices to associated products and perspectives.

Intermediate Learners at the Postsecondary Level

- Learners observe, analyze, and exchange information on patterns of behavior typical of their peers and other groups from the target cultures found in authentic materials such as video clips, blogs, and magazine and newspaper articles.
- Learners use culturally appropriate verbal and nonverbal behavior in daily activities among peers or mixed groups.

- Learners explore, analyze, and present to others how (and why) common cultural practices and procedures are carried out (e.g., how to set a table, how to participate in an election, how to accept or decline an invitation).
- Learners begin to adjust language, behaviors, and messages to acknowledge audiences with different cultural backgrounds.
- Learners role play a variety of situations from the target culture, using culturally appropriate behaviors and expressions.
- Learners suggest cultural triangles with reasons connecting practices to associated products and perspectives.
- Learners interpret authentic materials (e.g., short stories, videos, infographics, instruction booklets, magazine articles) to identify and analyze practices (e.g., respecting social media etiquette, finding a job, respecting the environment, dating, child rearing) that reflect perspectives of the target culture.

Sample Progress Indicators

ADVANCED RANGE LEARNERS

To interact with cultural competence and understanding

Advanced Learners

- Learners use formal and informal forms of address appropriately.
- Learners engage in conversations with native speakers in a culturally respectful way.

Advanced Learners in Middle School and High School

- Learners use culturally appropriate behaviors in a variety of situations in the target culture.
- Learners adjust language, behaviors, and messages to acknowledge audiences with different cultural backgrounds.
- Learners connect practices to associated products, giving evidence-based reasons for the perspectives proposed.

Advanced Learners at the Postsecondary Level

- Learners interact in a variety of peer- or mixed-group cultural activities, using appropriate verbal and nonverbal cues.
- Learners engage in discussions with native speakers using culturally appropriate behaviors and language to express agreement and disagreement.
- Learners identify, analyze, and discuss various patterns of behavior or interaction typical of the culture studied as represented in authentic materials (e.g., literary texts, films, social media, interviews, news stories).
- Learners prepare oral and written presentations with attention to the cultural background of the audience.
- Learners identify, examine, and analyze connections between socially accepted behavioral practices and cultural perspectives by conducting online and library research, observations, and interviews.

C RELATING CULTURAL PRODUCTS TO PERSPECTIVES

Learners use the language to investigate, explain, and reflect on the relationship between the products and perspectives of the culture studied.

This Standard focuses on the products of the culture studied and on how they reflect the perspectives of that culture. Products may be tangible (e.g., a painting, a cathedral, a piece of literature, a blog post, a pair of chopsticks) or intangible (e.g., an oral tale, a dance, a sacred ritual, a governmental body, educational institutions). Whatever the form of the product, its presence within the culture is required or justified by the underlying beliefs and values (perspectives) of that culture. Additionally, the use of the product is incorporated into one or more cultural practices.

For example, in the United States, youth has traditionally been valued more than old age (a perspective). As a result, products that purport to prolong youth and vitality (e.g., facial creams, high fiber cereals, Botox, fitness equipment, vitamin supplements) have become an integral part of our culture. At the same time, practices that are perceived as prolonging youth and health are encouraged: Children and adults faithfully exercise to music video workout routines or join fitness facilities; supermarket shoppers compare nutritional labels of food products prior to making selections; whole segments of the population invest in running shoes and exercise clothing (products); some consider plastic surgery and other medical procedures to look younger. But what are the perspectives toward youth/old age in the target culture? What products provide evidence of these attitudes? At all levels of language learning, students could consider using either the triangle in the Cultures Framework or advanced organizers (e.g., Venn diagram, chart, journal, word cloud generator) to record observations, reflections, and open questions as they use the language to increase their cultural understanding and competence.

Living rooms in many Moroccan homes are furnished with *sedari* (a product)—low sofas that surround three sides of the room with low, round tables placed before them. This arrangement reflects the high value placed on hospitality (a perspective) in Moroccan culture since guests can be seated comfortably for the long, leisurely multi-course meals that are served (a practice). For overnight guests, sedari can double as sleeping surfaces.

Sample Progress Indicators

NOVICE RANGE LEARNERS

To interact with cultural competence and understanding

Novice Learners

- Learners identify and observe tangible products of the culture such as toys, dress, homes, monuments, currency, famous people, and art.
- Learners identify, discuss, and produce types of artwork, crafts, or graphic representations enjoyed or made by their peer group within the target culture such as models of monuments, mosaics, murals, traditional recipes, ojos de dios, anime, henna tattoos.

Novice Learners in Elementary School

- Learners in Grades K–5 identify and tell the purpose of products of the target culture.
- Learners in Grades K–5 listen to or read about expressive products of the culture such as children's or traditional songs, selections from the literature commonly read and types of artwork enjoyed or produced by their peer group in the target culture.
- Learners in Grades K–5 illustrate products associated with the culture.
- Learners in Grades K–5 make simple cultural triangles showing the relationship of products, practices, and perspectives.

Novice Learners in Middle School and High School

- Learners give simple reasons for the role and importance of products from the target cultures.
- Learners listen to and/or read short poems, stories, plays from the target culture, identifying the author and country of origin.
- Learners listen to and/or sing songs from the target culture, identifying the musician and country of origin.
- Learners make simple cultural triangles connecting products to associated practices and possible perspectives.

Novice Learners at the Postsecondary Level

- Learners observe and demonstrate how products are used in the culture.
- Learners listen to and/or read short poems, stories, or plays from the target culture, identifying the author and country of origin.
- Learners watch video clips of commercials or television programs in order to identify products and their use in the target culture.
- Learners listen to and/or sing songs from the target culture, identifying the musician and country of origin.
- Learners create cultural triangles and describe the connections of products to associated practices and perspectives.

Sample Progress Indicators

INTERMEDIATE RANGE LEARNERS

To interact with cultural competence and understanding

Intermediate Learners

- Learners experience (read, listen to, observe, perform) expressive products of the culture (e.g., stories, poetry, music, paintings, dance, drama, and architecture) and explain the origin and importance of these products in today's culture.

Intermediate Learners in Elementary School

- Learners in Grades 3–5 search for, identify, and investigate the function of products (e.g., sports equipment, household items, tools, foods, clothing) of the culture studied compared to their function within the learners' homes and communities.

Intermediate Learners in Middle School and High School

- Learners identify and analyze cultural products found in literature, news stories, and films from the target culture.
- Learners create cultural triangles connecting products to associated practices along with suggested perspectives based on background information.

Intermediate Learners at the Postsecondary Level

- Learners identify, investigate, and analyze the function of everyday objects produced in the culture (e.g., household items, tools, foods, clothing).
- Learners compare and analyze perspectives reflected in news reports, social media, pamphlets, advertisements, legislation, etc.
- Learners identify and discuss perspectives reflected in creative works of the culture such as traditional and contemporary music, literature, dance, and art.

Sample Progress Indicators

ADVANCED RANGE LEARNERS

To interact with cultural competence and understanding

Advanced Learners in Middle School and High School

- Learners research in detail the role and importance of products from the target cultures.
- Learners identify and analyze the role and importance of cultural products found in literature, news stories, and film.
- Learners describe how some cultural products have changed or disappeared over time.
- Learners create cultural triangles connecting products to associated practices and giving evidence-based insights to the cultural perspective.

Advanced Learners at the Postsecondary Level

- Learners identify, discuss, and analyze social, economic, and political institutions, and explore relationships among these institutions and the perspectives of the culture.
- Learners identify, analyze, and discuss tangible and intangible products and their use as represented in authentic materials (e.g., literary texts, films, social media, interviews, news stories).
- Learners identify, examine, and analyze the relationship between cultural products and perspectives by conducting online and library research, observations, and interviews.

GOAL AREA: **C**ONNECTIONS

Connect with other disciplines and acquire information and diverse perspectives in order to use the language to function in academic and career-related situations

RATIONALE

Teaching and learning in the 21st century require that our students obtain a set of knowledge, skills, and literacies that will prepare them adequately for future education as well as life and work throughout the century ahead. Providing multiple opportunities for interdisciplinary learning is a critical component in the development of curriculum, instruction and assessment in all content areas at all grade levels. Language learning plays a key role by connecting with other disciplines either formally or informally, thereby expanding the educational experiences of all students. Knowledge is power, and extending student access to information and diverse perspectives through the use of another language and culture increases student ability to "know and do"— in both academic and career-related settings. Using this new language to access, manage, and effectively use information empowers students with knowledge, no matter what the topic or discipline. It also provides learners with skills and information that look beyond the limits of their formal educational experiences to help them become informed global citizens now and in the future.

In today's society, access to information takes on a multitude of forms that allows learning to occur at anytime and anywhere. Learners may view authentic news releases from countries around the world, or listen and watch live interviews with celebrities, journalists, or international leaders. Using available digital technology such as smartphones and tablets, they can access vast stores of information and entertainment from around the world while at home, in school, or in any other setting. Classroom instruction can guide learners to access the wide variety of sources available in the language. They may acquire information through live or technology-mediated personal conversations and interviews, as well as through authentic multimedia and print sources.

The conscious effort to connect the world language curriculum with other parts of students' academic lives opens doors to information and experiences that enrich the students' entire life and school experience, while at the same time increasing their skills in information, media, and technology literacy. These interdisciplinary connections, which add unique experiences and insights to the entire curriculum, flow into the language classroom from other content areas studied and also originate in the language classroom and may flow out to the classrooms of other subject areas as learners take the information acquired back to other classes.

DISCUSSION

Knowledge of another language and culture combines with the study of other disciplines to shift the focus from language acquisition to broader learning experiences and the acquisition of 21st century skills for the learner. Language used as a vehicle to teach content in this way helps students integrate the contributions from any discipline into a holistic and ever-expanding open system, while at the same time addressing skills such as critical thinking, problem solving, and information literacy. For example, while learning about the origins of the German classical music tradition, students with communicative competencies in the language deepen their understanding of a composer's works by reading segments of Bach's correspondence with contemporaries or excerpts from his diary describing his creative process. The same information could also be useful in other classes as students learn to forge connections across the disciplines, shifting emphasis from the learning of individual language pieces to recognition that language acquisition is a continuous process contributing to lifelong learning. Being able to identify key ideas and details in authentic sources in another language is a literacy skill directly related to many states' reading standards. Additionally, the growth of language study at the postsecondary level is directly connected to the combination of language with disciplines that have global implications or international connections. Learners in the 21st century must be prepared to live and work in a world in which global awareness and understanding are critical components to survival. Students who pursue the fields of journalism, political science, sciences, or the arts, for example, often have ambitions to work, conduct research, or live abroad. Frequently they acquire dual majors or minors in languages in order to interpret documents and exchange ideas with native speakers, which often constitute their primary reasons for continuing with the study of a language or beginning a new one. For other students, the connections between language learning and their fields of study may provide a secure foundation or scaffolding for a future career. To be competitive across the globe, learners in the United States need to match the preparation of learners from other countries, most of whom have experienced schooling that included many years of learning one or more additional languages.

Introducing learners to new content and perspectives through the language learners' access to new sources of information is the guiding principle for content-based courses, in which the goals are to increase knowledge and skill in a content area as well as in the language. Immersion and dual-language immersion programs in elementary schools, middle schools, or high schools are organized around connecting the development of performance in the new language with the development of the content area, such as mathematics, science, health, arts, physical education, or social studies. The curriculum of immersion and dual-language immersion programs is the grade-level content from other disciplines, with language as the means to acquire the knowledge and skills of the other disciplines. Likewise, at the postsecondary level, content-based courses provide a similar connection of content with language, providing additional opportunities to practice and improve language skills while acquiring the course content from another subject area, such as business, history, or media studies.

Taking the shift from teacher-directed to student-directed learning one more step, students use their developing language and cultural skills to go beyond the requirements for class work and pursue topics further for personal interest, unrelated to the limits of academic life. Today's technology provides them with easy access to any topic at any time of day or night. In this way, students become active global citizens who begin to nurture lifelong learning skills and lifelong language-using skills, the development of which are critical for all 21st century learners.

Although students entering the language classroom may have had no prior experience with language learning, they bring a wealth of experience and knowledge of the world around them, both in other areas of the school curriculum and from personal experience. Furthermore, those learners with language backgrounds other than English bring additional linguistic and cultural experiences to their classrooms. With one of the goals of language instruction being to "connect with other disciplines and acquire information and diverse perspectives," the teacher can use the classroom language learning experience to build upon what students already know in order to help prepare them "to use the language to function in academic and career-related situations" that they will encounter in our ever-changing global environment. Such activation of prior knowledge and experience can also occur in other learning environments outside the classroom (e.g., online, independent project-based, blended). Sometimes, language teachers may be hesitant to create interdisciplinary tasks or units, thinking, "I'm not a scientist or an art historian." The Connections goal area does not require expertise in other content areas; rather it seeks a teacher willing to help learners locate documents and other materials and to assist them with communicative tasks based upon the students' background knowledge and interests. In this way, language acquisition focuses on the broader education of students; it benefits their growth in non-language disciplines, encourages the transfer, enrichment, and strengthening of information; it helps students "learn how to learn"; it develops skills in critical thinking and creative problem solving.

Connections Standards

STANDARDS

 Making Connections

 Acquiring Information and Diverse Perspectives

The Connections goal includes two Standards. The first focuses on exploring content from other disciplines through the target language. The second focuses on information now available to the learner through the target language that adds one or more diverse perspectives not provided by multimedia and print sources available in the English language.

C MAKING CONNECTIONS

Learners build, reinforce, and expand their knowledge of other disciplines while using the language to develop critical thinking and to solve problems creatively.

Learning today is no longer restricted to a specific discipline; it has become interdisciplinary. Just as reading and the development of literacy skills, for example, are no longer the sole responsibility of the English language arts educators but rather are central to all aspects of the curriculum, so too does the study of world languages build upon the knowledge and skills that learners acquire in other subject areas. In addition, learners can relate the information studied in other subjects to their learning of the language and culture. This integration of knowledge and ideas in the Interpretive Mode of communication reinforces the literacy standards of most states and one aspect of a liberal arts education at the postsecondary level. Learners reinforce, expand, and deepen their understanding of and exposure to other areas of knowledge, even as they refine their communicative abilities and broaden their cultural understanding. The new information and concepts presented in one class become the basis of continued deeper learning in the language classroom, where learners use critical thinking and creative problem solving skills to make connections. A major focus of this Standard revolves around students learning how to communicate the content that they know in the English language in the three communicative modes of another language. In the lower elementary grades, for example, students in a science class are introduced to the range of vocabulary related to weather, seasons, and temperatures. At the same time, the language class continues this presentation with the months of the year, seasons, and weather vocabulary in the world language. By comparing the weather conditions in the target-language countries with those at home in interpersonal, interpretive, and/or presentational tasks, students have acquired new knowledge at the same time that they have reinforced their understanding of previously learned information. At secondary or postsecondary levels, learners may understand how the political process works in their country but not know how to describe it in the target language. As students learn useful terminology and how to express diverse perspectives in the target language, they can discuss their political system and also use video conferencing or exchange email messages with a peer from the target culture in order to compare systems.

Interdisciplinary reinforcement can occur at all levels of the school curriculum. At various stages, the language educator, for example, can teach more than names and events presented within the context of a unit in a history or geography class by introducing the language learners to journalistic accounts of historical events or literary depictions of individuals living at that time and available only through the target language. Learners can carry out research or web searches for target-language sites with specific information about an historical event or geographical location being studied in another class. Furthermore, in addition to the concepts and processes introduced in science and the achievements of artists and musicians studied in art, learners can read and respond to authentic descriptions of success and failure in biographical sketches of various historical figures, as well as the autobiographical accounts documented in personal letters and diaries of those individuals. Prior reading and discussion of various types of texts in classes of the English Department enable learners to have a better understanding of text types, genres, and literary conventions when they encounter similar texts in the world language classroom. Learners, who in a science class are investigating an environmental issue affecting major areas of the world (e.g., climate change), can build upon this knowledge by reading and discussing authentic articles about the issue in target-language media. Even the manipulations and story problems taught in math provide content and a basis for discussion and exploration in the language classroom, thereby building and expanding upon the original content. When integrated into the broader curriculum, language learning contributes to the entire educational experience of learners, preparing them to be ready for life and work in the 21st century.

Sample Progress Indicators

NOVICE RANGE LEARNERS

To connect with other disciplines and acquire information and diverse perspectives in order to use the language to function in academic and career-related situations

Novice Learners in Elementary School

- Learners in Grades K–2 identify and label items in the target language on charts and visuals used as instructional materials in other content areas, including weather, math facts, measurements, animals, musical instruments, or geographical formations.
- Learners in Grades 3–5 draw and mark maps of their cities, states, and of countries where the target language is used with civic and geographic features studied in other classes.
- Learners in Grades 3–5 use a website about the rainforest that was introduced in a science class to create a poster in the target language that highlights plants, animal life, and weather in the area.
- Learners in Grades 3–5 read or listen to stories from the target culture and compare them to familiar stories from the same genre (e.g., folklore, fables, myths, legends).

Novice Learners in Middle School and High School

- Learners use mathematics skills to convert U.S. dollars to the currencies of other countries in order to understand prices of items such as clothing, tickets, and restaurant meals.
- Learners use mathematics skills to convert weights and measures from the American system to the metric system in order to understand distances, quantities of fruits and vegetables, etc.
- Learners use science knowledge and skills to record daily temperatures and weather in different locations around the world, giving reasons for temperatures based on location and time of year.
- Learners use knowledge from health and science classes to compare healthy-eating recommendations using food pyramids or the equivalents from different countries.
- Learners use skills from social studies and English language arts to present short biographical sketches of people from the past and present who have had a positive influence locally and/or globally.

Novice Learners at the Postsecondary Level

- Learners identify, label, describe, and compare items in the target language on charts and visuals used as instructional materials in other content areas, such as mathematics, art, geography, music, or social sciences.
- Learners draw and mark maps (of places they live and places where the target language is spoken) with civic and geographic features studied in other classes.
- Learners read and view different text types and genres (with an emphasis on interpreting content).

Sample Progress Indicators

INTERMEDIATE RANGE LEARNERS

To connect with other disciplines and acquire information and diverse perspectives in order to use the language to function in academic and career-related situations

Intermediate Learners in Elementary School

- Learners in Grades 3–5 share information in the target language about topics from other school subjects, including geographical terms and concepts, historical facts and concepts, mathematical terms and problems, and scientific information.
- Learners in Grades 3–5 use their knowledge of history to create timelines of historic events in the countries where the target language is spoken.
- Learners in Grades 3–5 write original poems, stories, and plays using their understanding of the characteristics of these genres gained in English language arts.
- Learners in Grades 3–5 use their knowledge of geography to create maps of countries where the target language is spoken.

Intermediate Learners in Middle School and High School

- Learners seek out articles or multimedia in the target language on topics being studied in other classes and enter notes on main ideas in a journal.
- Learners make oral or written presentations in the target language on topics being studied in other classes.
- Learners describe and compare key characteristics of countries where the target language is spoken.
- Learners report on and evaluate the effectiveness of efforts to care for the environment in countries where the target language is spoken.
- Learners maintain a blog comparing attitudes and reactions to current events of global importance in countries where the target language is spoken
- Learners evaluate the role and importance of schooling for all children in countries where the target language is spoken.
- Learners use technology to present representative examples of contemporary culture (e.g., music, art, architecture) from countries where the target language is spoken.
- Learners research and compare how countries where the target language is spoken deal with water shortages.
- Learners research and report on contributions of the cultures that use the target language (e.g., Latin and Greek) to science, medicine, and government.

Intermediate Learners at the Postsecondary Level

- Learners prepare and present a concept in the target language that they studied in another academic subject (e.g., historical facts and concepts, mathematical terms and problems, scientific information).
- Learners draw on knowledge they have gained in another academic subject to discuss topics in the target language.
- Learners read, view, compare, and classify different text types and genres (with an emphasis on interpreting content and form).

Sample Progress Indicators

ADVANCED RANGE LEARNERS

To connect with other disciplines and acquire information and diverse perspectives in order to use the language to function in academic and career-related situations

Advanced Learners in Middle School and High School

- Learners write a critical analysis of a movie from a country where the target language is spoken.
- Learners use their knowledge of subjects taught in their schools to tutor English language learners whose first language is the target language.
- Learners use their knowledge of different forms of government to compare how leaders of countries where the target language is spoken are chosen or elected.
- Learners create an innovation/invention to improve the quality of life of people around the world.
- Learners write and produce an original play to highlight a challenge facing people in countries where the target language is spoken.

Advanced Learners at the Postsecondary Level

- Learners explore, discuss, and debate topics from other academic subjects, including political and historical concepts, worldwide health issues, and environmental concerns.
- Learners analyze and present information on a topic studied in other classes by conducting online and library research, observations, and interviews.
- Learners identify and analyze characteristics of different text types and genres.

C ACQUIRING INFORMATION AND DIVERSE PERSPECTIVES

Learners access and evaluate information and diverse perspectives that are available through the language and its cultures

As the level of students' performance and proficiency in language increases, they have expanding access to the target language's unique means of communication and ways of thinking. This access is provided through interpersonal interactions and authentic materials, both multimedia and print, prepared in the target language by and for native speakers. These materials—whether creative works, documentaries, or online information—provide unique perspectives not distorted by translation. These "texts" may not even be available in a translated format. Students broaden the sources of information available to them, which they can access effectively, evaluate critically, and use accurately. As 21st century learners, they have a "new window on the world," with 24/7 access through digital technology. In the earlier stages of language learning, they begin to examine a variety of sources intended for native speakers, and extract specific information and perspectives. They see how peers learn about particular topics or issues in a variety of materials and texts, be they presented in a school textbook, in media, or on a website; they identify how people in another country present common concepts or topics. How does a French writer describe Napoleon or a Modern Greek article treat the origins of democracy? How is a widely used product advertised in another country and how does this reflect and influence the language and culture associated with it? How do target language cultural perspectives influence an online recounting of a current U.S. event that is broadcast from the target language country? As students become more proficient users of the world language, they seek out additional materials of interest to them, analyze the content and cultural perspectives, compare them to information available in their own language, and assess linguistic and cultural similarities and differences.

Sample Progress Indicators

NOVICE RANGE LEARNERS

To connect with other disciplines and acquire information and diverse perspectives in order to use the language to function in academic and career-related situations

Novice Learners in Elementary School

- Learners in Grades K–5 read, listen to, or talk about age-appropriate school content such as ecology, social studies, sciences, the arts, physical education, and health.
- Learners in Grades K–5 expand vocabulary for working with school content through illustrated visuals (e.g., planets, anatomy, timelines of historical periods, maps).

Novice Learners in Middle School and High School

- Learners interpret the main idea(s) from infographics showing statistics such as numbers of endangered animals, changes in population of cities and countries, and popularity of various sports and leisure activities.

- Learners view video clips and identify ways that the people in the target cultures protect the environment on a daily basis.
- Learners identify the main idea(s) of current events reported in the news on the Internet from countries that speak the target language.
- Learners view websites of schools in countries where the target language is spoken to identify courses, schedules, and special projects, and compare the information to their school's website.

Novice Learners at the Postsecondary Level

- Learners explore instructional websites and materials created for speakers of the target language and identify the subject areas and topics (e.g., history lesson on immigration, a geography lesson on trade routes, a biology lesson on cell structure).
- Learners explore news media and identify the subject areas and topics.
- Learners discuss short texts and videos from the target culture.

Sample Progress Indicators

INTERMEDIATE RANGE LEARNERS

To connect with other disciplines and acquire information and diverse perspectives in order to use the language to function in academic and career-related situations

Intermediate Learners in Elementary School

- Learners in Grades 3–5 use sources intended for same-age speakers of the target language to prepare presentations on familiar topics.

Intermediate Learners in Middle School and High School

- Learners pull up a current event article or broadcast on the web in the target language and chart how it compares with the same event reported in the United States.
- Learners research how a major figure from history, science, or the arts is described in the target language and use it to expand what they already know.
- Learners access survey results about preferences related to daily life (e.g., music, leisure activities, movies) of people in countries where the target language is spoken and compare the results to preferences of people in their community.
- Learners view publicity for products sold in countries where the target language is spoken and compare the publicity to the way similar products are marketed in the United States.
- Learners compare news articles on front pages of newspapers from countries where the target language is spoken.
- Learners compare listings of houses for sale in countries where the target language is spoken in terms of what features are showcased, cost, size, and location.

Intermediate Learners at the Postsecondary Level

- Learners analyze instructional websites and materials created for speakers of the target language and compare them to instructional resources in the United States.

- Learners find, compare, and discuss coverage of current events in the target culture and in the United States.
- Learners present on an internationally known figure from history, science, or the arts using target language resources.

Sample Progress Indicators

ADVANCED RANGE LEARNERS

To connect with other disciplines and acquire information and diverse perspectives in order to use the language to function in academic and career-related situations

Advanced Learners in Middle School and High School

- Learners research an issue of global importance in order to provide insights from the perspective of a country or countries where the target language is spoken.
- Learners read a piece of literature in the target language and analyze the universality of the message.
- Learners prepare a virtual exhibit of artwork from a country where the target language is spoken, situating the contents historically, and explaining the importance of the artwork to the country of origin.

Advanced Learners at the Postsecondary Level

- Learners identify and analyze pedagogical approaches used in instructional websites and materials created for speakers of the target language.
- Learners discuss and analyze representations of pedagogical practices in literary texts and films.
- Learners research and debate global issues as represented in target language news sources with different political slants.
- Learners compare, analyze, and present on how and why advertisements for the same product differ in the target culture and the United States.

GOAL AREA: COMPARISONS

Develop insight into the nature of language and culture in order to interact with cultural competence

RATIONALE

Language learners discover and come to understand and use diverse patterns and perspectives inherent in both language systems and cultures in order to function competently in varied linguistic and cultural contexts. Through the study of a new language system and of how such a system expresses meanings in culturally appropriate ways, learners gain insights into the nature of language and the communicative functions of language in society, as well as the multifaceted nature of interaction between language and culture.

DISCUSSION

Research on the effects of second language learning indicates that learners are better able to reflect on their first language and culture after having experienced learning a second. Anecdotal evidence supports this idea that by engaging in comparisons between their native language and the language studied, learners come to develop a greater understanding of their own language and culture and of language and culture in the broadest sense. Study of a second language provides another path to understanding the role that language conventions, functions, and vocabulary play in communication and how languages often convey meaning in different ways. Similarly with cultural products, practices, and perspectives, learners often do not recognize and understand the cultural roots of many of the behaviors and beliefs in their own society until they see how these are manifested in another culture.

Some would argue that equivalent knowledge of language and cultural systems can be acquired in other types of courses at the secondary or postsecondary level (e.g., social studies or humanities, linguistics, anthropology). However, when learners try to make meaning and express themselves in another language and they participate in commu-

nicative interactions in another culture, their experiences provide evidence to verify or modify the concepts of language and culture that previously had only been studied. Byram (1997) argues that successful communication includes attention to the cultural knowledge and understandings that are an inseparable element of communication. By becoming skilled in how to express particular meanings in a second language, how to encode them linguistically, and how to recognize associated cultural norms and incorporate them appropriately into communication, students gain awareness of the nature of language itself and concurrently build their level of cultural competency.

For example, learners often come to the study of another language with the assumption that all languages are like their own. Soon, however, they discover categories that exist in other languages (e.g., grammatical gender) that do not exist in their own. They discover that elements to which they gave scant attention in their own language (e.g., word endings) may be quite important in another language. Moreover, they realize that what is appropriate in one cultural system (e.g., when and to whom to say thank you, when to use an imperative) often is not parallel in the other. These experiences direct attention to a comparison of language and cultural systems. In turn, such awareness enhances the ability not only to use the target language, but also to gain insights into the strategies their own language uses to communicate meaning. The Comparisons goal area is about much more than simply recognizing cognates or exploring a culture's variety of vocabulary for a particular phenomenon, such as for different types of precipitation. Comparisons gives attention to how language and culture combine to express concepts such as how time is divided or how relationships are expressed. This deeper understanding of expression through language and culture supports learners' development of literacy at the elementary, secondary, and postsecondary levels.

Whether or not learners continue the study of a particular language throughout their formal education, the understandings gained about the nature of language and its interaction with culture carry over into future circumstances where they, as learners and workers in the 21st century, will have the confidence and competence to interact in other cultural settings. Students learn ways of hypothesizing and making predictions about how language is likely to work in settings unfamiliar to them. They cease to make naive assumptions about other languages and cultures solely based upon knowledge of their own, and they learn to express and analyze similarities and differences between the two languages and cultures.

The long-term experience of studying another language leads learners to understand the nature of culture and to discover that other cultures view the world from a perspective different from their own. Learners view cultural practices, products, and perspectives in a new light as they probe apparently similar concepts in the target culture. For example, the word "bread" evokes certain images among American students based on its role and reality in our culture. These images cannot be automatically transferred to the second language. The appearance, taste, use, and perception of bread in another culture may be entirely different. When students understand that the target culture assigns new associations to the label "bread," they are drawn to examine this concept more closely in their native language. They begin to realize that language learning is not simply a matter of learning different vocabulary words, but of acquiring an entirely new set of cultural concepts associated with the words in order to communicate effectively in a manner that is culturally appropriate.

The study of another language and the resulting intercultural exploration expand a learner's view of the world. This study creates an awareness of the existence of alternative views of other cultures while at the same time providing insights into the learner's native language and culture. In addition, by comparing both cultural and linguistic systems and understanding the interconnections among systems, students develop skills in literacy, critical thinking, and problem solving in valuable and important ways.

Comparisons Standards

STANDARDS
Language Comparisons
Cultural Comparisons

The Comparisons goal includes two Standards. The first Standard focuses on the nature of language, the second on the concept of culture.

C LANGUAGE COMPARISONS

Learners use the language to investigate, explain, and reflect on the nature of language through comparisons of the language studied and their own.

This Standard focuses on the impact that learning the linguistic elements in a new language has on students' ability to examine their own language, and to develop hypotheses about the structure and use of languages. From the earliest language learning experiences, students can compare and contrast the two languages and the ways in which they express meaning in both sound and writing systems in all three modes of communication. As learners come to understand how language works in another language, their understanding of language conventions and functions expands. This awareness carries over to their first language as they apply this deeper understanding to improve their effectiveness at communicating and understanding messages. Additionally, learners acquire vocabulary in another language that often will aid them in determining the meaning of certain words in their first language. Words cannot always be translated literally because they carry different significance in other cultures, Certain expressions have no translation. Building such awareness develops the learners' skills in all the languages they may use in their life and work.

Sample Progress Indicators

NOVICE RANGE LEARNERS

To develop insight into the nature of language in order to interact with cultural competence

Novice Learners

- Learners cite and use examples of words that are similar in the language they are learning and their native language, and they pose guesses about why languages in general might need to borrow words.
- Learners identify cognates between the target language and their native language and cite the patterns that connect them, and they detect false cognates when the context in which they see them suggests a misfit.
- Learners inventory idiomatic expressions in both their native language and the language being learned and talk about how idiomatic expressions work in general.

Novice Learners in Elementary School

- Learners in Grades 3–5 observe and identify formal and informal forms of language in greetings and leave-takings.
- Learners in Grades 3–5 report differences and similarities between the sound and writing systems of their own language and the language being learned.

Novice Learners in Middle School and High School

- Learners compare word order in items such as the date and placement of descriptors.
- Learners observe formal and informal forms of language in greetings and leave-takings and try out expressions of politeness in other languages and their own.

- Learners report differences and similarities between the sound and writing systems of their own language and the language being learned.

Novice Learners at the Postsecondary Level

- Learners inventory and compare idiomatic expressions in the language they are learning and their own.
- Learners observe and compare registers of language (e.g., formal and informal) in greetings and leave-takings and other common social interactions in the language they are learning and their own.
- Learners identify similarities and differences between the sound and writing systems in the language they are learning and their own

Sample Progress Indicators

INTERMEDIATE RANGE LEARNERS

To develop insight into the nature of language in order to interact with cultural competence

Intermediate Learners in Elementary School

- Learners in Grades 3–5 match groups of people with ways of expressing respect and communicating status differences in their own language and the language they are learning.
- Learners in Grades 3–5 identify words in the target language that have no translation in English and vice versa.
- Learners in Grades 3–5 compare word order in the target language to English.
- Learners in Grades 3–5 notice how different time frames are expressed in the target language.

Intermediate Learners in Middle School and High School

- Learners hypothesize about the similarities of languages based on their awareness of cognates and similar idioms.
- Learners match groups of people with ways of expressing respect and communicating status differences in their own language and the language they are learning.
- Learners compare how different time frames are expressed in the target language and their native language and describe the shades of meaning expressed by such differences.

Intermediate Learners at the Postsecondary Level

- Learners identify and use borrowed words and cognates in the language they are learning and their own, and hypothesize about their origins.
- Learners compare and analyze idiomatic expressions in the language they are learning and their own, and hypothesize about their origins.
- Learners identify and compare language appropriate to specific social groups and situations in the language they are learning and their own.
- Learners identify patterns and explain discrepancies between the sound and writing systems in the language they are learning and their own.
- Learners compare syntax functions (e.g., word order and inflections) to express meaning in the target language and in English.

Sample Progress Indicators

To develop insight into the nature of language in order to interact with cultural competence

Advanced Learners in Middle School and High School

- Learners compare the choice and use of prepositions among languages.
- Learners recognize that cognates have the same as well as different meanings among languages and speculate about the evolution of language.
- Learners keep a journal of phrases and idioms that do not translate directly from one language to another.
- Learners analyze elements of the target language, such as time and tense, and comparable linguistic elements in English, and conjecture about how languages use forms to express time and tense relationships.
- Learners report on the relationship between word order and meaning and hypothesize on how this may or may not reflect the ways in which cultures organize information and view the world.
- Learners compare the writing system of the target language and their own. They also examine other writing systems and report about the nature of those writing systems (e.g., logographic, syllabic, alphabetic).

Advanced Learners at the Postsecondary Level

- Learners identify and analyze lexical and grammatical changes in the language they are learning and their own (e.g., disappearance of tenses, obsolescence, neologisms) and speculate about the evolution of language.
- Learners identify lexical and grammatical gaps between the language they are learning and their own and develop strategies for expressing nuance despite these gaps.
- Learners analyze and compare differences between spoken and written grammar and lexicon in the language they are learning and their own, taking into account audience, purpose, and genre.
- Learners identify, compare, and analyze sociolinguistic patterns in the language they are learning and their own by conducting online and library research, observations, and interviews.

C CULTURAL COMPARISONS

Learners use the language to investigate, explain, and reflect on the concept of culture through comparisons of the cultures studied and their own.

Inherent in learning a language is learning about one or more cultures associated with it. As learners expand their knowledge of cultures through language learning, they gain a deeper understanding of perspectives, practices, and products that are similar to and different from those in their own culture. They develop the ability to evaluate the similarities and differences found in multimedia and digital/print resources in the Interpretive Mode of communication. They learn to understand and incorporate cultural appropriateness in both the Interpersonal and Presentational Modes. Additionally, they learn to analyze and hypothesize about cultural systems in general and they develop a level of global awareness in which they become open and responsive to new and diverse perspectives. This Standard provides for the integration of investigative and reflective processes regarding cultures into instruction at all levels of learning.

Sample Progress Indicators

NOVICE RANGE LEARNERS

To develop insight into the nature of culture in order to interact with cultural competence

Novice Learners in Elementary School

- Learners in Grades K–2 appropriately use gestures used to greet friends, family, or new acquaintances.
- Learners in Grades K–2 compare and contrast tangible products (e.g., toys, sports, equipment, food) of the target cultures and their own.
- Learners in Grades 3–5 compare simple patterns of behavior or interaction in various cultural settings (e.g., transportation to school, eating habits).
- Learners in Grades 3–5 compare and contrast intangible products (e.g., rhymes, songs, folktales) of the target cultures and their own.

Novice Learners in Middle School and High School

- Learners compare games, stories, songs, and rhymes from their childhood to those in the target cultures.
- Learners compare daily routines in their culture and the target cultures.
- Learners compare celebrations (e.g., birthdays, holidays) in the target cultures to their own.
- Learners compare meal time in their culture and the target cultures.
- Learners compare places in a city where the target language is spoken to places in the city where they live.

Novice Learners at the Postsecondary Level

- Learners identify, describe, and compare/contrast products (e.g., tools, toys, clothing, homes, foods) and their use in the target cultures and their own.

- Learners observe, identify, and compare/contrast simple patterns of behavior or interaction in various settings in the target cultures and their own.
- Learners demonstrate and compare/contrast appropriate gestures and oral expressions for greetings, leave takings, and other common social interactions in the target cultures and their own.
- Learners identify and discuss similarities and differences in themes and techniques in creative works from the target cultures and their own.

Sample Progress Indicators

INTERMEDIATE RANGE LEARNERS

To develop insight into the nature of culture in order to interact with cultural competence

Intermediate Learners in Elementary School

- Learners in Grades 3–5 fill in a Venn diagram that compares sample daily activities in the target culture and their own.
- Learners in Grades 3–5 speculate on why certain products originate in and/or are important to particular cultures by analyzing selected products from the target cultures and their own.
- Learners in Grades 3–5 hypothesize about the relationship between cultural perspectives and practices (e.g., holidays, celebrations, work habits, play) by analyzing selected practices from the target cultures and their own.

Intermediate Learners in Middle School and High School

- Learners hypothesize about the relationship between cultural perspectives and expressive products (e.g., music, visual arts, forms of literature) by analyzing selected products from the target cultures and their own.
- Learners compare and contrast the role and importance of family in the target cultures to their own.
- Learners compare and contrast school schedules, course offerings, and attitudes toward school in the target cultures to their own.
- Learners compare and contrast the role of social networking in the target culture and their own.
- Learners compare and contrast career choices and preparation in the target cultures to their own.
- Learners compare and contrast entertainment and leisure options in the target cultures and their own.

Intermediate Learners at the Postsecondary Level

- Learners document and contrast verbal and nonverbal behavior in daily activities among peers or mixed groups in the target cultures and their own.
- Learners identify, investigate, and compare/contrast the function of everyday objects (e.g., household items, tools, foods, clothing) produced in the target cultures and their own.

- Learners compare and contrast authentic materials (e.g., creative works, news, social media) from the target cultures and their own to identify and analyze practices and perspectives of the target cultures and their own.

Sample Progress Indicators

ADVANCED RANGE LEARNERS

To develop insight into the nature of culture in order to interact with cultural competence

Advanced Learners in Middle School and High School

- Learners compare and contrast the value placed on work and leisure time in the target cultures and their own.
- Learners compare and contrast behaviors related to health and wellness in the target cultures and their own.
- Learners compare and contrast attitudes toward youth and aging in the target cultures and their own.
- Learners compare and contrast the importance placed on individual needs versus community/global needs in the target cultures and their own.

Advanced Learners at the Postsecondary Level

- Learners report on the relationship between word order and meaning and hypothesize on how this may or may not reflect the ways in which cultures organize information and view the world.
- Learners hypothesize about the origins and use of idioms as reflections of culture, citing examples from the language and cultures being studied and their own.
- Learners compare cultural nuances of meanings of words, idioms, and vocal inflections in the target language and their own.
- Learners identify, discuss, and analyze social, economic, and political institutions and related perspectives in the target cultures and their own.
- Learners identify, analyze, and discuss tangible and intangible products and their use in the target cultures and their own, as represented in authentic materials (e.g., literary texts, films, social media, interviews, news stories).
- Learners identify, examine, and analyze the relationship between cultural products, practices, and perspectives in the target cultures and their own by conducting research, observations, and interviews.

GOAL AREA: COMMUNITIES

Communicate and interact with cultural competence in order to participate in multilingual communities at home and around the world

RATIONALE

The increasing interconnectedness of the world's economy requires the United States to continue shifting from a manufacturing-based economy to one increasingly based on information, technology, and service in global environments. As businesses from China to Chile expand both domestic and international markets, U.S. citizens must become proficient in other languages and adept at understanding and communicating appropriately in cultural contexts. Changing demographics within the United States also require these language and cultural skills within both large and small communities throughout the country. Additionally, social networking has become truly international in nature, whether as a conduit for personal exchanges or for educational, political, or professional purposes. Now more than ever, Americans want and need to access directly knowledge and information generated by other countries and cultures in order to be active participants and partners in the global community.

Language proficiency and cultural competence are developed and sustained by continued opportunities to learn and use a language over a long period of time. Moreover, learners tend to become more engaged in and excited about language learning in any environment when they see immediate applications beyond the classroom for the competencies they learn. They find that their ability to communicate in other languages and to interact in culturally appropriate ways better prepares them for school and community service projects, enables them to expand their employment opportunities both at home and abroad, and allows them as lifelong learners to pursue their own interests for personal benefit. Ultimately, as a result of their ability to communicate in other languages, learners realize the interdependence of people throughout the world.

The Communities goal combines elements from each of the other four goal areas. Once again, careful application of the components of language and culture are vital for learner success. The Standards in this goal are dependent not only on appropriate language use at each level of language learning, but also on the ability to apply knowledge of the relationships among perspectives, products, and practices of a culture, the ability to connect with other disciplines, and the development of insight into one's own language and culture. In many ways, the Communities Standards are the ultimate rationale for learning the languages of the world in order to prepare learners to participate effectively in communities, both at home and across the globe. Additionally, recent research on university student attitudes toward the Standards indicates that the Communities Standards rank highest for them (Magnan, Murphy, Sahakyan, & Kim, 2012). Learners do not need to wait until they reach a high level of proficiency to use the language beyond the classroom; they must have opportunities throughout the language learning experience to practice and exhibit their communicative and cultural competencies with speakers of the language, in both individual and community settings that occur face-to-face or in a virtual environment

DISCUSSION

A rapidly changing American society and a world of instant global communications require a workforce that meets the needs of global economies and consumers who may not speak English. A heightened need for national security places additional demands on today's workforce. Knowledge of another language and culture positions workers to serve the needs of a global society by interacting effectively and competently with others around the world. In other countries, knowing at least two (if not three or four) languages is more common than in the United States, where language learning is sometimes layered by starting the study of a second language by early adolescence and a third language by later adolescence. Recognizing the need for a productive and competitive workforce in the global environment, schools across our nation are emphasizing a curriculum that incorporates 21st century skills and literacy in order to better prepare students for postsecondary educational opportunities and the world in which they will live and work. Colleges and universities are beginning to add programs that link an international focus to existing majors such as in business or sociology, expand languages for special purposes such as health careers or social work, and create interdisciplinary majors that include language study and internships abroad. These educational efforts extend directly to the language classroom, preparing competent and self-confident learners skilled not only in communication, critical thinking, problem solving, and creativity, but also in information, media, and technology literacy. In order to live and work in multilingual communities both at home and around the globe, today's learners will require the combined resources and expertise provided by schools; postsecondary institutions; businesses; governments at local, state, and national levels; and public and private organizations.

The Communities goal area includes attention to identifying one's goals and motivation for language learning and reflecting on progress toward reaching those goals. Using the learners' future use of intercultural communicative competence as a rationale for language learning and expansion of program offerings means that educators need to provide learners the means to be successful as they use language in their life and work. Educators need to consider the learners' goals for language learning—enjoyment, enrichment, or advancement—when making choices of content and classroom activities, thus creating a learner-centered language experience. In addition, learners need to know they are making progress toward their goals. The use of portfolios, learning targets stated in terms of what the learner "can do" with the language, and performance demonstrations based on applications of language and cultural competence help learners chart their progress with meaningful evidence.

Some learners are fortunate to have direct access to multilingual communities through their home backgrounds or local environment; all learners benefit from an awareness of the many communities in the United States where English and other languages are spoken—communities such as the Arabic-speaking communities in Michigan, the French-speaking Cajun areas of Louisiana, the German areas of the Texas Hill Country, the Italian communities of the Northeast, the Spanish-speaking communities of the Southeast and Southwest, and the Asian neighborhoods of the West Coast or New York City. Language learners develop a keener awareness of cultures that better equips them to participate with cultural competence in the multilingual communities that exist in the United States and abroad. The Communities goal area, however, should not be narrowly interpreted as referring only to opportunities for learners to physically travel abroad, enter a nearby community, or engage in a field trip for interaction with speakers of other languages. The virtual world reached via ever-increasing technology provides all learners—individually, in pairs or small groups, or as an entire classroom or school—with multiple opportunities for interaction with peers and others who speak the language they are learning. In this manner, learners can communicate with speakers in multilingual communities essentially anytime and anywhere. Through all types of digital and print media, we now have direct links with the entire contemporary world. Competence in more than one language and knowledge of other cultures empowers learners to communicate more effectively in the various environments that they will experience during their lifetime.

Communities Standards

STANDARDS

 School and Global Communities

 Lifelong Learning

The Communities goal includes two Standards. The first emphasizes active use of the target language to collaborate face-to-face and virtually, while the second focuses on goal setting to achieve personal enrichment and interests.

SCHOOL AND GLOBAL COMMUNITIES

Learners use the language both within and beyond the classroom to interact and collaborate in their community and the globalized world.

This Standard focuses on language as a tool for communication with speakers of the language throughout one's life and work: in schools and communities both within the United States and around the globe. In instructional settings, learners share their knowledge of language and culture with classmates and other language learners, as well as with educators, administrators, other staff members, and the educational institution as a whole. Institutions from elementary schools through graduate programs can also form virtual partnerships with individual students, classrooms, or entire school communities in another country, interacting on a regular basis through digital media tools available to them. Such partnerships may lead to collaboration to solve problems that transcend borders, participation in service learning in the local community, or sharing understandings of culture with one another. At any level of language learning, learners can engage in language- and culture-related events and projects within both real and virtual communities, at both the local and global level. As learners gain communicative abilities and increase their cultural understandings, they can apply what they are learning in the language to advance their communication with others and to pursue cultural or interdisciplinary goals. They come to realize the advantages inherent in being able to communicate in more than one language and they develop an understanding of the power of language. In our global economies, well-developed language and cultural applications increase not only the marketability of the employee, but also the ability of the employer to meet the expectations of the customer. As students experience increased opportunities to use language in response to real-world needs and interests, they seek out situations and environments in which they can apply their competencies beyond the school setting.

Sample Progress Indicators

NOVICE RANGE LEARNERS

To communicate and interact with cultural competence in order to participate in multilingual communities at home and around the world

Novice Learners

- Learners write and illustrate short stories to present to others.
- Learners perform for school, campus, or community celebrations.

Novice Learners in Elementary School

- Learners in Grades K–5 identify places that another language is used and attempt to interact with the language in some way (e.g., finding products in the language at a grocery store, attempting to speak to a community member in a library or restaurant).
- Learners in Grades 3–5 access relationships with speakers of the language either in person or via texting, email, social media forums, or voice chats.
- Learners in Grades 3–5 identify professions that require proficiency in another language.
- Learners in Grades 3–5 conduct online research and report on a cultural event or a school topic.

Novice Learners in Middle School and High School

- Learners communicate on a personal level with speakers of the language in person or via email, video chats, instant messaging, and shared video clips.
- Learners identify professions which require proficiency in another language.
- Learners create imaginary situations to role play interactions that might take place in a community setting.
- Learners do WebQuests and report on a cultural event or a school topic.

Novice Learners at the Postsecondary Level

- Learners exchange basic information about themselves, their studies, or their family, with speakers of the target language and/or students in other classes, in face-to-face or virtual settings (e.g., social media, instant messaging, video conferencing).
- Learners identify professions of interest to them that require proficiency in another language.
- Learners simulate interactions that might take place in a community setting.
- Learners write and illustrate short texts intended for a specific audience in collaboration with students in other classes.
- Learners prepare a group presentation or performance for a school, campus, or community event.

Sample Progress Indicators

INTERMEDIATE RANGE LEARNERS

To communicate and interact with cultural competence in order to participate in multilingual communities at home and around the world

Intermediate Learners in Elementary School

- Learners interact with members of the local community or with contacts made electronically to hear how they use the language in their various fields of work.
- Learners in Grades 3–5 participate in club activities that benefit the school or community.
- Learners travel to museums to add to their understanding of aspects of the cultures they have studied.

Intermediate Learners in Middle School and High School

- Learners discuss their preferences in leisure activities and current events, in written form or orally, with peers.
- Learners discuss steps to becoming a professional in a field requiring the ability to communicate in the target language.
- Learners present information gained from a native speaker about a cultural event or a topic of interest.
- Learners use their knowledge of the target language to tutor English language learners who speak the target language.
- Learners discuss their preferences concerning leisure activities and current events, in written form or orally, with peers who speak the language.

- Learners interact with members of the local community or with contacts made electronically to hear how they use the language in their various fields of work.
- Learners participate in language club activities which benefit the school or community.
- Learners write and illustrate stories to present to others.
- Learners perform for a school or community celebration.
- Learners travel to museums and re-enactments to add to their understanding of aspects of the cultures they have studied.

Intermediate Learners at the Postsecondary Level

- Learners discuss topics of personal interest through interpersonal oral or written exchanges with speakers of the target language and/or students in other classes, in face-to-face or virtual settings (e.g., social media, instant messaging, video conferencing).
- Learners interview members of communities, whether local or beyond, about how they use their knowledge of language personally and professionally, in face-to-face or virtual settings.
- Learners solicit, organize, and present information from a speaker of the target language about a cultural event or a topic of interest.
- Learners participate in language club activities that benefit the school, community, or other organizations.
- Learners travel to sites within the target cultures to add to their understanding of aspects of the cultures they have studied.

Sample Progress Indicators

ADVANCED RANGE LEARNERS

To communicate and interact with cultural competence in order to participate in multilingual communities at home and around the world

Advanced Learners in Middle School and High School

- Learners communicate orally or in writing with members of the other culture regarding topics of personal interest, community issues, or world concern.
- Learners participate in a career exploration or school-to-work project which requires proficiency in the language and culture.
- Learners use community resources to research a topic related to culture and/or language study.
- Learners design and organize a multimedia presentation about the language and culture to present to others.
- Learners participate in language club activities which benefit the school or community.
- Learners write and illustrate stories to present to others.
- Learners read, add information, and monitor edits on wikis in the target language.
- Learners provide service to the community by interpreting the target language at school, clinics, or daycare centers.

Advanced Learners at the Postsecondary Level

- Learners discuss and express opinions on current events and issues through interpersonal oral or written exchanges with speakers of the target language and/or students in other classes, in face-to-face or virtual settings (e.g., social media, instant messaging, video conferencing).

- Learners volunteer for a community organization, participate in a career exploration or school-to-work project, or complete an internship that requires proficiency in the language and culture.
- Learners use community resources in addition to library and online resources to research a topic related to culture and/or language study.
- Learners initiate and organize club activities that benefit the school, community, or other organizations.
- Learners write and illustrate stories to present to others.
- Learners conduct research in the target language or assist in the translation of resources for the benefit of a community organization.

C LIFELONG LEARNING

Learners set goals and reflect on their progress in using language for enjoyment, enrichment, and advancement

Language is an avenue to information and interpersonal relationships. Each day, millions of Americans spend their leisure time reading, listening to music and podcasts, viewing videos, films and television programs, surfing the Internet, and interacting with each other both face-to-face and in virtual environments. As students develop new levels of comfort with a world language, they can use these everyday skills and activities to access various entertainment and information sources available to speakers of the other language, thereby enriching their personal lives as they continue to learn. Some learners may have opportunities to travel to communities or countries where the language is used extensively and, through these experiences, further develop their language skills and cultural competence. Others may explore opportunities for personal enrichment and/or professional advancement through online and digital resources. Maintaining and increasing their proficiency and cultural knowledge prepares all learners to live and work in the increasingly multilingual communities of the 21st century.

Learners need to know that they are making progress toward these motivating goals. Such evidence needs to be based on clear learning targets based on the Communication Standards and demonstrated in contexts involving the other four Cs of the World-Readiness Standards goal areas. Learners need evidence from their learning that provides indicators of progress along the continuum of proficiency from Novice, to Intermediate, on to Advanced, and toward Superior. Educators assist learners to reflect on and measure their progress by providing feedback related to the targeted performance range for the current course or for learning experiences such as an internship abroad.

Sample Progress Indicators

NOVICE RANGE LEARNERS

To communicate and interact with cultural competence in order to participate in multilingual communities at home and around the world

Novice Learners in Elementary School

- Learners in Grades K–5 interpret materials and/or use media from the language and culture for enjoyment.
- Learners in Grades K–5 play sports or games from the culture.
- Learners in Grades K–5 exchange information about topics of personal interest.
- Learners in Grades K–5 plan real or imaginary travel.
- Learners in Grades K–5 attend or use media to view cultural events and social activities.
- Learners in Grades K–5 listen to music, sing songs, or play musical instruments from the target culture.
- Learners in Grades K–5 create can-do statements with the help of their teachers of what they want to communicate in the target language for each unit of instruction.
- Learners in Grades K–5 collect evidence showing that they have achieved the can-do statements for each unit.

Novice Learners in Middle School and High School

- Learners use the NCSSFL-ACTFL Can-Do Global Benchmarks to set SMART goals (specific, measurable, attainable, relevant, and timebound) to monitor and reflect on their progress in communication skills.
- Learners collect evidence showing that they have achieved the SMART goals they have set for each unit of instruction.
- Learners interpret materials and/or use media from the language and culture for enjoyment.
- Learners play sports or games from the culture.
- Learners exchange information about topics of personal interest.
- Learners plan real or imaginary travel.
- Learners attend or view via media cultural events and social activities.
- Learners listen to music, sing songs, or play musical instruments from the target culture.
- Learners explore the Internet to find sites of personal interest where they can use the language they are learning to maintain and increase their communication skills.

Novice Learners at the Postsecondary Level

- Learners use the NCSSFL-ACTFL Can-Do Global Benchmarks to set SMART goals (specific, measurable, attainable, relevant, and timebound) to monitor and reflect on their progress in communication skills.
- Learners collect evidence showing that they have achieved the SMART goals they have set for each unit of instruction.
- Learners seek out and explore authentic materials in the target language related to their hobbies, goals, and interests, and expand their vocabulary in these areas.
- Learners learn sports or games played in the target culture.
- Learners use online resources in the target language to plan travel.
- Learners attend or view cultural events and social activities.
- Learners listen to music, sing songs, or play musical instruments from the target culture.
- Learners explore the Internet to find sites of personal interest where they can use the language they are learning to maintain and increase their communication skills.
- Learners travel to museums or sites studied to add to their understanding of aspects of the cultures they have studied.

Sample Progress Indicators

INTERMEDIATE RANGE LEARNERS

To communicate and interact with cultural competence in order to participate in multilingual communities at home and around the world

Intermediate Learners in Elementary School

- Learners in Grades 3–5 create can-do statements with the help of their teachers of what they want to communicate in the target language for each unit of instruction.
- Learners in Grades 3–5 collect evidence showing that they have achieved the can-do statements for each unit.
- Learners in Grades 3–5 consult various sources in the language to obtain information on topics of personal interest.

- Learners in Grades 3–5 play sports or games from the culture.
- Learners in Grades 3–5 exchange information around topics of personal interest.
- Learners in Grades 3–5 use various media from the language and culture for entertainment.
- Learners in Grades 3–5 attend or use media to view cultural events and social activities.
- Learners in Grades 3–5 listen to music, sing songs, or play musical instruments from the target culture.

Intermediate Learners in Middle School and High School

- Learners use the NCSSFL-ACTFL Can-Do Global Benchmarks to set SMART goals (specific, measurable, attainable, relevant, and timebound) to monitor and reflect on their progress in communication skills.
- Learners collect evidence showing that they have achieved the SMART goals they have set for each unit of instruction.
- Learners consult various sources in the language to obtain information on topics of personal interest.
- Learners play sports or games from the culture.
- Learners exchange information around topics of personal interest.
- Learners use various media from the language and culture for entertainment.
- Learners attend or use media to view cultural events and social activities.
- Learners listen to music, sing songs, or play musical instruments from the target culture.
- Learners explore the Internet to find sites of personal interest where they can use the language they are learning to maintain and increase their communication skills.

Intermediate Learners at the Postsecondary Level

- Learners use the NCSSFL-ACTFL Can-Do Global Benchmarks to set SMART goals (specific, measurable, attainable, relevant, and timebound) to monitor and reflect on their progress in communication skills.
- Learners collect evidence showing that they have achieved the SMART goals they have set for each unit of instruction.
- Learners seek out and interact with speakers of the language who share similar hobbies, goals and interests, in face-to-face or virtual settings.
- Learners expand their knowledge and keep up with current events through target language resources.
- Learners follow and participate in sports or games played in the target culture.
- Learners join community or international groups that organize cultural events and social activities.
- Learners access news and entertainment media in the target language.
- Learners explore the Internet to find sites of personal interest where they can use the language they are learning to maintain and increase their communication skills.

Sample Progress Indicators

ADVANCED RANGE LEARNERS

To communicate and interact with cultural competence in order to participate in multilingual communities at home and around the world

Advanced Learners in Middle School and High School

- Learners use the NCSSFL-ACTFL Can-Do Global Benchmarks to set SMART goals (specific, measurable, attainable, relevant, and timebound) to monitor and reflect on their progress in communication skills.
- Learners collect evidence showing that they have achieved the SMART goals they have set for each unit of instruction.
- Learners consult various sources in the language to obtain information on topics of personal interest.
- Learners play sports or games from the culture.
- Learners read and/or use various media from the language and culture for entertainment or personal growth.
- Learners establish and/or maintain interpersonal relations with speakers of the language.
- Learners attend or use media to view cultural events and social activities.
- Learners listen to music, sing songs, or play musical instruments from the target culture.
- Learners explore the Internet to find sites of personal interest where they can use the language they are learning to maintain and increase their communication skills

Advanced Learners at the Postsecondary Level

- Learners use the NCSSFL-ACTFL Can-Do Global Benchmarks to set SMART goals (specific, measurable, attainable, relevant, and timebound) to monitor and reflect on their progress in communication skills.
- Learners collect evidence showing that they have achieved the SMART goals they have set for each unit of instruction.
- Learners regularly consult target language resources for personal enrichment, entertainment, and professional advancement
- Learners regularly interact with speakers of the language in face-to-face or virtual settings.
- Learners help organize and participate in cultural events and social activities.
- Learners travel to places where the language is spoken and/or host visits by speakers of the language.
- Learners explore the Internet to find sites of personal interest where they can use the language they are learning to maintain and increase their communication skills.

CONCLUSION

The challenge and opportunity of writing standards for language learners is a professionally fulfilling process for all involved. From the beginning of the project, the Standards Task Force recognized the responsibility it had in attempting to represent the ideas and opinions of professionals in the field. The members of the original task force, all practicing educators, tried to envision these Standards in use with all learners. In the almost two decades that have passed since the initial publication of the National Standards, districts, language departments and postsecondary programs have used the standards as a basis for designing curriculum, assessment, and professional development. The survey conducted of language professionals implementing the National Standards (Phillips & Abbott, 2011) over a 3-year period affirmed that the Standards have had major impact on the goals of language instruction as well as the conduct of learning in classrooms. As the Standards are refreshed and reintroduced to the profession, adding language that reflects 21st century teaching and learning plus years of experience using the Standards to focus and improve language learning, the 5 Cs of Communication, Cultures, Connections, Comparisons, and Communities continue to provide a unifying vision for language educators and learners.

Since their original publication, the Standards have had a transformative impact on language learning. Examples include the following:

- Standards now apply to pre-K–16 language learning and are for learners in elementary, middle, and high schools, and postsecondary colleges and universities.
- Language-specific standards exist for 14 languages and more are in development by national organizations and educators of those languages.
- Standards are reflected in numerous related educational initiatives that encompass language learning, including: the Council for the Accreditation of Educator Preparation (CAEP), formerly the National Council on the Accreditation of Teacher Education (NCATE); National Board for Professional Teaching Standards (NBPTS); Advanced Placement (AP) language courses; and the 21st Century Skills Map for World Languages.
- Textbooks and supplementary materials make reference to the Standards and a video library of standards-based classroom instruction was created by the Annenberg Foundation.
- New assessments are built upon frameworks grounded in the Standards such as the Integrated Performance Assessment (IPA), AP exams, and the ACTFL Assessment of Performance toward Proficiency in Languages (AAPPL).

Additionally, many articles have appeared in professional journals, magazines, and newsletters to report on research and practice using the Standards; conference presentations have occurred at every level, from local informal groups to national meetings. The Standards will remain a work in progress, needing to be regularly revisited and refreshed as necessary in light of new research and national initiatives. When first designed, there was no Skype or Facebook or YouTube. Video streaming was not smooth or reliable. Neither students nor their teachers were using the Internet as a major source of authentic materials. The access that technology now provides adds to the global communicative possibilities of the language classroom. The future holds even more possibilities. These World-Readiness Standards for Learning Languages, in the spirit of educational reform, set challenges for education institutions and educators, for parents and communities, and certainly for learners. Furthermore, this is not an impossible dream, for all the components that support these Standards currently exist and are accessible. All stake-holders need to collaborate to guarantee that these components to implement the Standards exist in all schools for all learners.

The World-Readiness Standards for Learning Languages have the power to act as beacons, as guidelines, for both short-and long-range planning across all levels of education: pre-K, elementary, secondary, and postsecondary.

LEARNING SCENARIOS

Following are a series of Sample Learning Scenarios in which classroom activities that reflect the Standards are described. The scenarios have been collected from teachers throughout the country and reflect a wide variety of programs, languages, geographic locations, and school settings. The scenarios should be considered illustrative examples of teaching and learning which incorporate the Standards. Those Standards applied in the scenario are highlighted along with a reflection which highlights the "weave" of the scenario, including the curricular elements, such as the language system, communication strategies, culture, learning strategies, other subject areas, critical thinking skills, and technology. The reflection also contains suggestions for adapting or extending the learning activities.

ARTS AND CRAFTS

Students of Italian are studying the crafts of Italy with an emphasis on the products of the different geographic regions (e.g., glass in Venice, alabaster sculpture in Volterra, ceramics in Orvieto, and inlaid wood in Sorrento). Students discuss the differences between arts and crafts, the lifestyles of the people who create or use the crafts, and the information one can learn about a craftsperson from examining his/her work. As an adjunct to this unit, students participate in an Aesthetic Institute unit on the dance called "Quilts" by the Tennessee Dance Theater. This work takes its inspiration from the patterns created by traditional American quilts and from the stories of the people who created them. The students are able to approach this work as a nonverbal extension of the "message" of the craftsperson, and another way to communicate the "passing down" of skills and knowledge through the generations.

TARGETED STANDARDS	REFLECTION
C Interpersonal Communication	Students discuss Italian and American crafts in the target language.
C Interpretive Communication	Students read and view videos on various craftspersons in Italy and interpret that information.
C Presentational Communication	Students present their interpretations of perceptions on the crafts and craftspersons studied.
C Relating Cultural Practices to Perspectives	Students identify characteristics of Italian life that gave rise to the targeted crafts.
C Relating Cultural Products to Perspectives	Students learn about the practical and aesthetic development of crafts in Italian culture by examining the products.
C Making Connections	Students reinforce content from their social studies, art, and dance classes.

TARGETED STANDARDS	REFLECTION
Acquiring Information and Diverse Perspectives	Students learn about the lives of craftspersons from authentic sources.
Cultural Comparisons	Students are able to give historically and sociologically correct information on targeted crafts in Italy and the United States; students discuss the artistic and social dynamics of cultures.
School and Global Communities	Students work with visiting artists.
Lifelong Learning	Students gain appreciation for artistry and craftsmanship.

This scenario touches upon the Standards in all five goal areas. Because all cultures have unique forms of craftsmanship, this scenario can be adapted for all languages. Similarly, the focus on crafts means that the unit can be adapted for a variety of age groups and levels of language competency. By including works such as "Quilts," students gain an entry point in the performing arts with the benefit of professional artists in the classroom.

BREAD AND CHOCOLATE

Third grade students studying French listen as the teacher describes foods typically eaten in France and typically eaten in the United States, such as *pain au chocolat* and sourdough bread with peanut butter. The students sample some food brought by the teacher. They share their impressions, describing the food in French and commenting on how it tastes. Generally, students take a piece of the *pain au chocolat*, and a couple of them like the new taste. Three students decide they don't care for the new taste. When the time comes for other students to try something new, most of them decide they won't like it and decline the offer. The teacher then asks who would like peanut butter and bread, and the whole class finds the offer irresistible. While the students are enjoying their peanut butter and bread, they learn from the teacher that most people in France would not enjoy this combination of foods. The students compare the tastes of the French and Americans and discuss the differences in food preferences. They are surprised to learn that something they consider to be tasty is not necessarily considered so by others. Some of the students then ask to try the *pain au chocolat* to experience something new.

TARGETED STANDARDS	REFLECTION
Interpersonal Communication	Students share their opinions about some foods from France and from the United States.
Relating Cultural Products to Perspectives	Students encounter a new aspect of culture that they would not otherwise know.
Cultural Comparisons	Students express their impressions of similarities and differences between some sampled foods from France and from the United States.

This activity addresses three goals. The students describe the foods and express their likes and dislikes in trying something new. They then compare their reactions to a new taste and to a food with which they are familiar. Finally, they discuss in English how people enjoy different things, and they express their surprise that something that is generally liked in one culture is not shared by another. Similar activities can be implemented using different aspects of culture. In order to avoid stereotyping, it should be noted that customs and preferences may vary within a culture.

BUTTERFLIES

Students at Sanchez Elementary School are fascinated by the yearly migration of butterflies. Their interest is channeled into an expansive interdisciplinary learning project. The art teacher helps them make butterflies from origami and tissue paper. In language arts, students are doing research and writing a report on the butterfly. Social studies classes are coloring maps showing the flight path of the monarch butterfly, while math teachers are constructing butterfly shapes to study symmetry. Students in science are learning about the life cycle of a butterfly. Even in health and physical education, Coach Garcia is teaching his students how to do the butterfly stroke and how to use a butterfly band aid. Señorita Rodriguez teaches her students the names for the various parts of the butterfly in Spanish using the samples provided by the art teacher. Students point to the different colors as she calls them out in the target language. Students may also show and tell about their butterflies using familiar adjectives to describe them and identifying the six stages of their life cycle. Working in pairs, students use the cardinal numbers to trace the migration of the monarch butterfly on a map, as well as to provide information regarding shape, color, size, and symmetry. Working in cooperative groups, students are asked to compose a verse about the butterfly. The project culminates with a field trip to a local museum of natural science to observe butterflies in their natural habitat.

TARGETED STANDARDS	REFLECTION
C Interpersonal Communication	Students use the language to identify parts of the butterfly and answer questions.
C Presentational Communication	Students tell about their butterflies and compose a verse about them.
C Making Connections	Students further their knowledge of butterflies in an interdisciplinary fashion.

This is an example of an integrated curriculum in which each subject seeks to provide learning opportunities for students around a common theme. The learning throughout the day is then reinforced for students, not only through different disciplines, but also through different learning modalities. This interdisciplinary aspect is particularly pertinent to language learning so that students make connections among the disciplines and see an immediate use and application for the other language. This approach is most easily accomplished now in the elementary school setting, but it can be used effectively at the middle and high schools with appropriate planning.

CHINESE CALENDAR

In Ms. Chen-Lin's Chinese class of eighth graders are learning about the Chinese calendar. Students listen to the folkloric tale of how the years got their names, which the teacher explains by using story cards. The students then use artistic expression to recall the details of the story by making posters that announce the race of the 12 animals in the story. They are encouraged to include on their poster the date, time, location, and prize in Chinese. On the next day, the class explores the importance of a calendar in the students' own culture and in others. The students discuss the differences found in the Chinese and American calendars. They then make a calendar using Chinese characters to be used in their homes. They include birthdays, family celebrations, school activities, and other special events.

TARGETED STANDARDS	REFLECTION
C Interpretive Communication	Students comprehend the story about the Chinese calendar.
C Relating Cultural Products to Perspectives	Students read about and discuss expressive products of the culture.
C Cultural Comparisons	Students compare and contrast calendars from the two cultures.

In this activity the students understand the calendar explanation more easily because the teacher accompanies the explanation with visuals. The use of artistic expression to check for their understanding allows students with various learning styles to be successful in showing what they understood from the story. The follow-up discussion helps students reflect on the importance of a calendar within a culture and the role that the calendar plays in American culture.

COMMUNITY PROJECT

As a part of a larger school-wide community service project, students at Forest Park Middle School discussed the ways that foreign visitors could be made comfortable in a new community, welcomed by merchants, and encouraged to use municipal services. They concluded that making signs in various languages would demonstrate a community's invitation to visitors to use the services. An eighth grade Spanish class chose the public library as the venue for their work. Working in pairs, partners assembled a list of vocabulary words and then made a directory of places and references where certain items could be found in the library. In addition, they prepared a list of useful expressions that are applicable to library users. Partners then compared and contrasted their individual lists and reported to the whole class; after a brainstorming session, students produced a final list of relevant vocabulary and phrases. The project culminated in the creation of brochures and posters to illustrate useful expressions and designate sections of the library. Finished posters were first displayed in the school building during Foreign Language Week, before being permanently installed in the community library. Spanish brochures were made available to visitors at the reference desk.

TARGETED STANDARDS	REFLECTION
C Presentational Communication	Students create brochures for the library.
C School and Global Communities	Students participate in an activity that benefits the community.

This activity is an example of student use of the language beyond the school setting. Assisting students in identifying and implementing community activities in which they use the language makes the learning relevant to students and helps them envision how they may be able to use the language in their personal lives in the future. Making the directory and signs for the public library would involve students' attention to the language system as any public signs should contain correct spelling and should accurately reflect how language structures are "telescoped." Students would also need to show attention to the cultures reflected in the communities so that appropriate vocabulary would be used.

COMMUNITY SERVICE PROJECT

Members of the Spanish Club at Sanchez High School undertake the clean-up of the old Spanish cemetery a few blocks from the school as their community project. On their first day at the cemetery, they are amazed at the names, birth and death dates, epitaphs, and other information inscribed on the tombstones. The history teacher becomes involved by having her students trace the historical background of some of the names inscribed on the tombstones. The art teacher has her students prepare pencil drawings of the cemetery and create "charcoal shadings/impressions" of interesting tombstones. Students from Spanish classes interview community members in Spanish to obtain a historical perspective. They also read and study about the Day of the Dead (*El Día de los Muertos*). They follow class discussions of ancient and modern death rituals in Spanish-speaking countries with further study of the verbs "to die" and "to be born," and the numbers up to 1000.

TARGETED STANDARDS	REFLECTION
Interpersonal Communication	Students conduct interviews with members of the Hispanic community.
Making Connections	Students further their knowledge of another discipline.
Cultural Comparisons	Students compare and contrast death rituals.
School and Global Communities	Students participate in a club activity which benefits the community.

This is an example of students' use of the language beyond the school setting in an activity that expands the knowledge of the students and benefits the community. The cultural and linguistic elements of the activity ensure that students are enhancing their knowledge in both of these areas. Class discussion will include the most effective use of language dictionaries and the linguistic issues involved in literal understanding of the epitaphs. This project may be easily expanded by comparing the information about the culture with death rituals and practices in various communities in the United States.

CULTURAL COMPARISONS

Students in Ms. Gadbois' French II class at Central High School received an article, written for a teen magazine in France, about a crime that occurred in the United States and the unusual sentence given to the criminals. The students discuss the crime, the pros and cons of each possible legal punishment, the view of the French writer toward the event, and how the same crime was treated in the American press. As a follow-up, students write a summary of the article.

TARGETED STANDARDS	REFLECTION
C Interpretive Communication	Students comprehend the principal elements of non-fiction articles on a topic of current importance.
C Cultural Comparisons	Students discuss the point of view of the French author and compare it to the American viewpoint.

This activity offers students the opportunity to view an event through the cultural perspective of a speaker of another language. It helps students to realize that the same event may be portrayed quite differently based on the cultural background of the reporter. By using the authentic source, students read an article that is aimed at their age group and concerns a topic with which they are all familiar. The article could also be the starting point of a discussion of idioms and vocabulary pertinent to an adolescent audience.

CULTURAL OBSERVATION

In trying to help students understand the similarities and differences between German and American cultures, students in Fresno are asked by their teacher, Ms. Koopman, to view a series of 10 slides depicting cultural diversity in Germany. The students study each slide for one minute and note what they see. In groups, the students discuss their observations and each group then reveals three observations to the whole class. They view the slides a second time and their teacher relates to the class the exact nature of each picture. The students then reevaluate their original observations and talk about the varied attitudes found in their own and in German culture. Ms. Koopman then asks the students to keep a journal over the next two-week period in which they jot down various observations about cultural diversity within either the German or U.S. culture. The students are also asked to draw a political cartoon which illustrates the misunderstandings between two cultures.

TARGETED STANDARDS	REFLECTION
C Interpersonal Communication	Students discuss their reactions to the slides in groups and write down their observations.
C Presentational Communication	Students present a political cartoon representing cultural diversity.
C Cultural Comparisons	Students demonstrate an understanding of how different cultures view diversity.

This type of activity could be used to discuss a variety of topics, such as how people live, dietary habits, dress, and expressive art forms from the culture studied. It could be done with students from elementary school, middle school, or high school with varying degrees of sophistication depending on the developmental level of the students. The final part of the activity, drawing the political cartoon, brings students' higher level thinking skills into play as they must synthesize the activity into a humorous setting.

DAILY SCHEDULES

The students in Monsieur Joseph's seventh grade French class have been learning to describe their daily routines. In their math class, they have been working with percentages, collecting and organizing data, graphing the data, and interpreting the data provided by the graphs. They have also been corresponding via email with epals in Dakar, Senegal. M. Joseph asks students to determine the amount of time they spend each day eating, sleeping, watching TV, and studying (in school or at home). Students determine what percentage of the school day they spend on each of these activities and display the information on a circle graph, labeling the graph in French. Students then work in groups of four to compare data on their graphs. Students take turns interpreting the graph of the person on their right, comparing the data on their own graph to that of the other person. At the end of the activity, each student provides a statement that summarizes what the group found and dictates this information to the group recorder. On a subsequent day, students use information they have received through correspondence with epals in Dakar to reflect upon how their daily schedules and allotment of time compare with those of their peers in Senegal.

TARGETED STANDARDS	REFLECTION
Interpersonal Communication	Students work collaboratively in groups.
Interpretive Communication	Students comprehend their email messages from Dakar.
Presentational Communication	Students present information about themselves to their group.
Relating Cultural Practices to Perspectives	Students learn about the practices of the students from Dakar.
Making Connections	Students make connections between the skills they are learning in math and their French class.
Cultural Comparisons	Students compare and contrast the use of time by the students in Dakar with their own.
School and Global Communities	Students use the language beyond their own community.

This activity exemplifies how skills learned in one class can be reinforced in the language class by developing meaningful activities with practical applications for students. Middle school students are focused on their lives and the lives of their peers. This activity takes that natural interest of the student and channels it into a learning activity. This might also be an opportunity for the students to focus on the language structures involved in making comparisons in French.

DIEGO RIVERA

The cultural focus of the fourth grade Spanish class at Perkins Elementary School is Mexico. Prior to Diego Rivera's birthday, the class begins its unit based on the book *Diego* by Jan Winters. The teacher uses props and pictures to introduce unfamiliar vocabulary. Strategies such as Teaching Proficiency through Reading and Storytelling (TPRS), active listening, and question/answer activities are used to practice new vocabulary. Students use a map of Mexico to lead into the setting of the story. Students participate in a pair activity in which they instruct their partners, using a map and a toy airplane, to travel to the areas within Mexico that are important to the story and to understand the general orientation of those areas within the country. The teacher reads the story to the students several times. They illustrate and label selected scenes from the book, orally tell the story in sequence, and participate in time line and story mapping activities after the readings. The teacher shares with the students many examples of Diego Rivera's works. In small groups, they talk about what they like and do not like about the paintings, and they make lists of the topics depicted in the murals. The students create a mural with the art teacher based on the time line of Diego Rivera's life that reflects the sequence of their own lives. The language teacher facilitates the writing of a language experience story about the mural.

TARGETED STANDARDS	REFLECTION
Interpersonal Communication	Students engage in conversations about the story and Diego Rivera's works.
Interpretive Communication	Students comprehend the story when told by the teacher.
Presentational Communication	Students present information about the story.
Relating Cultural Practices to Perspectives	Students understand the cultural practices depicted in the works of Rivera.
Relating Cultural Products to Perspectives	Students become familiar with cultural products of Mexico (Rivera's murals).
Making Connections	Students make connections with other disciplines (art and social studies).
Cultural Comparisons	Students compare the life of Rivera with their own.

The basis for this activity is a work of children's literature based on the life of Diego Rivera. The techniques used by the teacher help students in an elementary FLES (Foreign Language in the Elementary School) program to understand the story. Learners make a connection between the artist's life and medium (murals) with their own life. Once again, the element of culture undergirds the context for this activity.

DINOSAURS

Kindergarteners at Rockbridge Elementary School are learning about dinosaurs with the typical fascination that this subject holds for young students. To complement their study of this topic, their teacher, Señora Matos, develops an activity for their FLES Spanish class with the cooperation of the art teacher. The students use construction paper to create a "Jurassic Mountain" in the classroom. In Spanish, they learn the words for *tree, mountain,* and other elements of their newly created environment. However, the teacher and students realize that something is missing: the dinosaurs. Students are asked to bring dinosaurs to school, and on the next day their "Jurassic Mountain" and two other tables are covered with dinosaurs. After learning the vocabulary in Spanish, the students identify and describe the dinosaurs and classify them by size, color, and other characteristics (gentle, fierce, etc.). Students then make brightly colored papier-mâché dinosaurs as well as dioramas reflecting the appropriate habitat for their dinosaurs. At the end of the week, Señora Matos has 21 diverse dinosaur dioramas, labeled in Spanish, to be shared with the school community.

TARGETED STANDARDS	REFLECTION
Interpretive Communication	Students understand the presentations of their classmates.
Presentational Communication	Students present information about their dinosaurs to fellow students.
Making Connections	Students reinforce and further their knowledge of prehistoric life.
School and Global Communities	Students use the language within the school setting.

This scenario could occur in any language with beginners at any grade level. The content would depend on the setting. The scenario might be played out using such topics as mythical figures, medieval artisan shops, or signs of the Chinese calendar in cooperation with teachers from various disciplines. The curricular weave is highlighted in the classification aspect of the activity in which students use critical thinking skills to organize and classify the dinosaurs. By encouraging students to ask and answer questions of each other, a focus on the Interpersonal Communication Standard, could be added to this activity.

DOING BUSINESS IN JAPAN

Students in Mariko Jeffrey's seventh grade Japanese class have been learning Japanese for 6 years through a partial-immersion program. In this activity, they begin by comparing the geography of Japan with the geography of the United States and the various regional products that are available for export to other countries. Based on this information, the teacher leads the students in a discussion of products whose import and export might benefit Japanese and American businesses. From this discussion, the teacher introduces the concept of the business card in Japanese society. Using authentic business cards, students identify the types of information included. They then make their own business cards representing a product that they had suggested for export. As a final activity, students pair up and introduce themselves and their product to each other.

TARGETED STANDARDS	REFLECTION
Interpersonal Communication	Students introduce themselves and their products to each other.
Interpretive Communication	Students demonstrate understanding of the teacher's explanations of the concept of the business card.
Relating Cultural Practices to Perspectives	Students learn about the practice of exchanging business cards in Japanese society.
Relating Cultural Products to Perspectives	Students understand the role of the business card and its use.
Making Connections	Students learn about the various geographic features of Japan and their influence on products that are available for export.

In this scenario, the students are involved in making the transition from an elementary partial-immersion program that focused on the elementary school curriculum to the high school language program. Students have a high level of listening and speaking proficiency and use that to introduce themselves and present product information. The teacher also focuses on the writing system as students need to systematically increase their knowledge of Kanji. There may also be grammatical features that need to be discussed more formally than would be addressed in the elementary school program. The geographic and economic concepts maintain students' interest as they increase their knowledge of Japanese language and culture.

FAIRY TALES

Each student in the Spanish III class at Shiloh High School reads a fairy tale from the target language culture in order to gather information and learn the vocabulary used in this type of story. After researching the vocabulary and studying the grammatical structures, students select the information that best expresses the principal ideas and themes of the story. Students summarize this information in phrases to demonstrate an understanding of the material. Then, key verbs in the story are used in sentences. Once this activity is finished, students begin an analysis of the story in the target language. They discuss physical appearance, intellectual traits, cultural practices and perspectives, and notable characteristics of the characters. They also talk about the characters' contributions to the story, the principal and secondary themes, and the climax of the story. In pairs or small groups, students select two stories to be combined into one for the purpose of creating one new story. In order to write the new fairy tale, students discuss the characters and their function in the new story, organize the characters to fit the new theme and plot, evaluate the new situations, and provide solutions to problems and conflicts. Upon completion, each new story is then presented orally through dramatizations. Students use puppets, marionettes, or a felt board for story telling. The written story is presented in the form of a pop-up book where each page has three-dimensional illustrations and a text for narration. Each new story is videotaped for enjoyment and error correction. The written and videotaped versions of the fairy tales are kept as a part of the classroom library.

TARGETED STANDARDS	REFLECTION
C Interpretive Communication	Students read the fairy tale.
C Presentational Communication	Students present their fairy tale orally or through dramatization.
C School and Global Communities	Students write stories to present to others.

In this activity, students focus on the language structures and vocabulary within the authentic cultural context of a fairy tale. The process of putting the characters and themes into a new story involves the use of higher-level thinking skills. The presentation aspect is a good vehicle for student expression in the target language. The students also focus as a group on error correction by pointing out common errors made on the tapes. This might be appropriately done before the final version is filmed or taped.

CULTURAL PERSPECTIVES

Viewing a film in another language is an effective way to expose students to native speakers and to provide them with an opportunity to see how people live and react to the world they inhabit. *Indochine*, a French film which takes place in Indochina in the early 1920s to 1950s, is the story of a French rubber plantation owner, her family, and how French colonialism, communism, and other social and political events completely changed their lives. Before viewing the film, Mrs. Gibson's III and IV classes at Meadowcreek High School had a short discussion of Indochina at the time period of the film. It was important to establish the history and context of France's involvement and colonial experience in Indochina. The film, 2½ hours long, was shown as 10-15 minute segments each day followed by students filling out a graphic organizer to help them discuss what happened in that segment, then skipping over a section of the film for the next day's viewing and starting the next class with the teacher providing a written summary of the part skipped. In this way the students experienced the entire film in short segments over the course of one week, but did not spend three full days just viewing the film. After the film, students wrote a "response to literature" essay, in which they summarized their personal reaction to the film, its themes, and what new information and perspectives they had gained.

TARGETED STANDARDS	REFLECTION
C Interpretive Communication	Students view the film in French.
C Presentational Communication	Students write a reaction to the film.
C Relating Cultural Practices to Perspectives	Students gain insight into the patterns of behavior of the culture studied.
C Making Connections	Students further their knowledge of geography and history.
C Lifelong Learning	Students view a French feature film.

Viewing a full-length feature film can be daunting to language learners. In this example, the teacher has effectively divided the film into smaller segments with a discussion following each part. By setting the stage with the necessary background information, the teacher prepares the students to comprehend the film effectively. Students gain a level of confidence about functioning within a culture other than their own when their classroom learning experiences include activities such as this one.

GEOGRAPHY

In many school districts, third graders study other countries and cultures in social studies. By third grade, students understand the concepts of countries and continents. They know that many cultures are represented in the United States, and they are beginning to explore the diversity of the peoples of the world. Classroom teachers may choose to study a country in Asia or Africa as a part of the third grade social studies program. The language teacher can then present information about these world regions in the language class. For example, third graders studying Spanish at Naubuc Elementary School are also studying about the country of Ghana. Even though Ghana is not a Spanish-speaking country, students use Spanish to review world geography and locate Ghana on the African continent. The language teacher, Ms. Trusz, reinforces concepts already presented in social studies by teaching the vocabulary for the products, languages, animals, weather, geography, etc., of the country. Because Ghana is a country near the equator, and many Spanish-speaking people also live in equatorial countries, the vocabulary and concepts learned about Africa reinforce information already presented about the target culture. After being asked to brainstorm the similarities and differences among a community in Ghana, a Spanish-speaking community, and their local community, the students then write several paragraphs or develop projects about Ghana in Spanish which depict these similarities and differences. The language class includes students who speak Spanish as a first language. These students are able to enrich the authenticity of the language experience by adding their insights about the local Spanish-speaking community.

TARGETED STANDARDS	REFLECTION
Interpretive Communication	Students comprehend information about life in Ghana.
Presentational Communication	Students prepare projects and/or writing assignments for others to read.
Relating Cultural Practices to Perspectives	Students learn about the cultural practices of the communities.
Relating Cultural Products to Perspectives	Students learn about the cultural products of the communities.
Making Connections	Students further their understanding of world geography.
Cultural Comparisons	Students compare and contrast life in the local community, a Spanish-speaking community, and a community in Ghana.
School and Global Communities	Students use the language in the school setting.

This scenario relates what students learn in other disciplines and what they know about the culture of the language studied to their own life experiences. The fact that native speakers of Spanish are in the class allows the teacher to vary the assignment in order to challenge students. Other topics which might be addressed in this way include schooling, professions, and political systems. The use of a Venn diagram to help students visualize the organization of the similarities and differences among the communities would encourage these young students to use high level thinking skills in organizing their writing. By including Ghana, the Spanish-speaking community, and the local community in the discussion, the students are developing a multicultural perspective that can be applied to other settings.

LANGUAGE COMMUNITIES

Second year French students at Central High School listen to Monsieur Mensah, a substitute teacher in the school, describe his country, Togo, and its customs in the target language. Each student asks him two questions in French about a topic of particular interest to him/her. The visit is a success for both the visitor and the students. The guest is impressed by the courtesy of the class and the students' ability to comprehend his language, and the students marvel at the story of Togo, its importance in African history, and the fact that it is a popular country in attracting tourists. M. Mensah is an excellent role model as he explains the importance of French in his country, why he speaks it, the fact that his parents do not, and what opportunities it has presented to him in his lifetime. The students then prepare a résumé of what they have learned from M. Mensah in either in either video or written essay form. As a follow up, the students will research Togo via the Internet.

TARGETED STANDARDS	REFLECTION
C Interpersonal Communication	Students ask questions of the visitor.
C Interpretive Communication	Students comprehend the main ideas and some details.
C Making Connections	Students further their knowledge of an African country.
C School and Global Communities	Students communicate with members of the other culture.

The teacher might use this opportunity to review the language system in terms of asking questions, since the students developed questions to ask the visitor. The focus on interrogatives would help students refine their language skills in this area. The follow-up using the Internet would bring technology into the extension activity.

HOCKEY LESSON

Students from Plainview Kennedy High School learn about hockey firsthand from players for the New York Islanders who were born in Canada and were raised speaking French. Teacher David Graham wants to give his students a French lesson in hockey so he arranges for two players from the Islanders team to address his French students. The students spend several hours asking questions in French about professional hockey and the players' personal lives.

Afterwards, the students attend a specially priced hockey game with their parents in which the Islanders play opposite the Montreal Canadiens.

TARGETED STANDARDS	REFLECTION
C Interpersonal Communication	Students ask questions of the players.
C School and Global Communities	Students participate in a community activity.
C Lifelong Learning	Students show evidence of enjoyment of the language.

The teacher reports that several months after this activity the students are still excited about the experience. Having the students attend the game in addition to the assembly was important, he says, because "it takes the kids' interest in sports and ties it directly to learning a language." This activity could be replicated in Spanish classes with Hispanic members of soccer teams or in German classes by interviews with German tennis players.

INTERNATIONAL SCIENCE

Students in Ms. Welch's biology class in Jessamine County High School have been working in teams to study viruses, conducting experiments in the lab while researching a particular strain of viral infection. One team has become intrigued by the work done at the Pasteur Institute in the exploration of the virus which causes AIDS. Maria and John are both taking French and know that they could probably add significantly to the biology class if they were able to contribute information about the Institute and its work. They obtain the address of the Institute through a Minitel (national database in France) search using John's computer at home. Not finding an email address, the pair decides to write the Institute and request information regarding work on the virus. The jointly composed letter becomes an entry in each of their French writing portfolios. After 4 long weeks, a packet of materials finally arrives. The pair is disappointed to find that the items in the packet are almost all in English. Discussion of the virus has become old news in the biology class as new topics have replaced virus study. John and Maria, however, are intrigued to find that the French perspective of the history of the discovery of the HIV virus differs subtly from what they had assumed after reading in biology class. Ms. Welch is pleased with their initiative, interested in the perspective they noticed about the research, and invites the students to share the information with classmates during a formal presentation to the rest of the class. Rather than focusing exclusively on viral infections, the ensuing discussion centers on competition in science, the scientific process, and reasons why much of the technical work in the field is written in English.

TARGETED STANDARDS	REFLECTION
Interpersonal Communication	Students compose a letter to send to the Pasteur Institute.
Interpretive Communication	Students read the few materials in French that they received from the Institute.
Making Connections	Students further their knowledge of the virus.
Acquiring Information and Diverse Perspectives	Students realize that the French perspective of the discovery of the virus varies from the American.

This activity is an example of students learning to view a topic through the perspective of another culture. After realizing that the history of the HIV virus was treated slightly differently in an article written in French, students could then identify a series of current events and analyze how these topics are handled by the press in various French-speaking countries. Students would use critical thinking skills to conduct the analyses of the various treatments.

JOURNAL WRITING

Students in the German III class at Las Cruces High School write entries in a journal four times a week. The journals are written outside of class, and students are free to write on topics of their own interest. One of their weekly journal entries is the discussion of an article of the students' choice. The school has a subscription to a German newspaper and to a weekly magazine, and issues are available for the students to take home. Some of the students use the Internet to find reading materials to review in their journals. The language department has access to *Deutsche Welle TV*. Their teacher records various programs which the students can then view at home and discuss in their weekly journals.

TARGETED STANDARDS	REFLECTION
Interpretive Communication	Students interpret articles and videos.
Presentational Communication	Students write reactions to the articles and videos.
Lifelong Learning	Students use media from the culture to obtain information on topics of personal interest.

To target the Presentational Communication Standard, the students could prepare an analysis of current events, and time could be set aside each week for students to share what they have read or viewed with their classmates. The students could also use these authentic documents to identify, discuss, and analyze such products of the culture as social, economic, and political institutions and thus target the Cultural Products Standard. The teacher also helps students focus on individual difficulties with using the language system by highlighting common errors in language usage when reacting to the students' journal entries. This would not be done by correcting errors for the student, but by calling attention to areas in which students need to improve. Peer editing is another effective way to help students improve writing skills by providing an audience other than the teacher for the student writing.

SISTER SCHOOL PROJECT

Madame Nelson's eighth graders rush into the classroom and eagerly gather at the computer to check for responses from their French epals. They have been able to correspond with 13-year-olds from a school in southern France by using the the Internet to connect with their peers in France. Mme Nelson's students are in their second year of French, so they are able to write to their French counterparts and ask questions about a typical school day, life in French communities, and what students there like to do for fun. They are also able to share this information about themselves in French. Today in class they download the French students' responses, then read the responses and formulate questions and answers for their next communication. Approximately half of the class period is spent on this activity. Then their attention turns to the next assignment, in which Mme Nelson gives each group a specific amount of money and they must decide how they will spend it while dining in Paris. They return to the Internet and access a list of restaurants in Paris and the menus of the fare offered. They are able to select menu items for a full French meal and calculate the amount spent in euros. The groups then evaluate the work of the others by ascertaining how balanced the meal was, how close the group came to spending the amount assigned, and whether an appropriate tip was given. The assignment for tonight is to calculate the equivalency of the amount each group spent in euros with U.S. dollars.

TARGETED STANDARDS	REFLECTION
C Interpersonal Communication	Students correspond with French epals.
C Making Connections	Students discuss the nutritional value of their meal and calculate expenses.
C Acquiring Information and Diverse Perspectives	Using technology, students access and use menus from French restaurants.
C School and Global Communities	Students use the language to discuss the project with their classmates.
C Lifelong Learning	Students show evidence of being able to order from a French menu.

This scenario exemplifies how technology facilitates language learning and plays a role in motivating students to use the language with peers. It also highlights the visionary aspect of the Standards. Technology plays a critical role in bringing native speakers and current information from the culture into the classroom. The teacher can enhance the language competence of students by focusing on communication strategies from the "weave" of language learning, so that students will know how to keep the communication going with their peers even if they are not certain how to express themselves.

MYSTERY CLASS

To review material learned the previous year, students in this German II class are asked by their teacher, Sue Webber, to write a description of themselves as well as information about where they live and their interests. The students then photograph themselves holding items that represent their hobby (e.g., fishing pole and net for salmon). Each student's picture is numbered, and the package of descriptions and pictures is sent electronically to the partner school. The receiving school's students read each letter and match the letter with the picture. They also guess at the location of the mystery school based on the information given by the students in their letters that might suggest region or place. Since the school communicates on the Internet, it is a quick process to see if the students guess correctly.

TARGETED STANDARDS	REFLECTION
C Presentational Communication	Students write information about themselves and where they live.
C School and Global Communities	Students use their language to interact beyond their own school setting.

This activity combines technology with a review of basic structures from German I and the high interest provided by communicating information with peers. This activity provides the basis for long-term communication among the students in which they may share cultural information such as use of the telephone, doors open vs. doors closed in a home, parental attention to teens' whereabouts, etc. The students are able to reflect on their own culture by reading what German students say about the differences they see between the cultures.

NEW YEAR'S CELEBRATION

High school students are preparing for a Chinese New Year's Celebration in their second-year Chinese class. They read materials in Chinese and in English on the celebration, which explains several aspects of the tradition. They also view a videotape explaining the extended celebration and preparation for it. The students then discuss the perspectives, products, and practices depicted in the film and reading materials, comparing their own experiences celebrating an American New Year. Earlier in the year they had made origami "good luck wishers" and red envelopes for money. One day is spent designing cards and invitations for the New Year's celebration. Special attention is paid not only to words for the event but also to the appropriate colors. They learn how to care for the calligraphy set, grinding ink and washing brushes, and they practice the basic strokes before writing the characters on rice paper. The calligraphy work is then displayed in the school library prior to the celebration. The classes then listen and learn the words to a New Year's song and practice dance steps. After making a lion's head, they perform the lion dance for the school and in the community.

TARGETED STANDARDS	REFLECTION
Interpersonal Communication	Students work together to plan the celebration.
Interpretive Communication	Students read and view materials in the language.
Relating Cultural Practices to Perspectives	Students learn about and participate in the celebration.
Relating Cultural Products to Perspectives	Students experience expressive products of the culture.
Acquiring Information and Diverse Perspectives	Students learn through the language about the significance of the celebration.
Language Comparisons	Students analyze New Year's greetings in the two cultures.
Cultural Comparisons	Students compare celebrations.
School and Global Communities	Students interact with each other and perform in the community.

This scenario addresses Standards in each of the five goal areas. The activities can be done within a variety of cultural contexts focusing on celebrations such as birthdays, Halloween and *El Día de los Muertos*, or Christmas. This scenario could be adapted to accommodate students in elementary and middle school programs. The focus on comparing and contrasting New Year's celebrations brings critical thinking skills into play, undergirded by cultural knowledge.

NEWSCAST

In the Spanish II classes in Williamston High School, students work in groups to write, produce, and videotape a 15- to 20-minute news show that includes current events; a live, on-the-scene report; weather; sports; and commercials. The news events include items from the Spanish-speaking world, the United States, and state and local areas.

TARGETED STANDARDS	REFLECTION
Interpersonal Communication	Students work in groups to produce the newscast.
Presentational Communication	Students present the newscast.
Relating Cultural Practices to Perspectives	Students reflect a perspective from the culture studied in the news stories.
Making Connections	Students develop news items using information from many fields.
School and Global Communities	Students create a context for using the language in the classroom.
Lifelong Learning	Students develop insights necessary for media literacy.

If the students were asked to view recorded newscasts and commercials from two Spanish-speaking countries and use them as models for their project, an emphasis could be placed on the Interpretive Communication Standard and the Acquiring Information Standard. By watching target language broadcasts, students are acquiring information in a form that is not available to them in English. The Language Comparisons Standard could be included by having students view newscasts and compare and contrast language styles. Students could also be asked to note cultural similarities and differences in the videotapes they viewed. This type of preparation for the project would also provide the opportunity to target the Cultural Products Standard, with students analyzing a product of the culture studied.

NEWSPAPER

Señor Fernandez's students listened to a presentation from a professional journalist on publishing the *Mundo Hispánico* in Atlanta. The guest speaker described the process leading up to the publication of an issue in Spanish. The students take notes during this presentation, which is conducted in Spanish. Small groups of students select specific tasks listed by the guest speaker as necessary for the production of their newspaper: editorials, interviews, entertainment highlights, cartoon strips, "Querida Carmen" (similar to "Dear Abby"), sports summaries, and a horoscope. In addition, each student writes a short story. Students are not only required to prepare the information assigned to them but also to present updates on their progress to the whole class. The students produce a Spanish newspaper. They work collectively on editing, re-writes, and format. Three students work at the computers. The students are very proud of their finished product and share the Spanish edition with other classes.

TARGETED STANDARDS	REFLECTION
C Interpretive Communication	Students listen to the presentation of the professional journalist and take notes.
C Presentational Communication	Students write an article for a student publication.
C Making Connections	Students further their understanding of media literacy.
C School and Global Communities	Students interact with members of the local community involved in a variety of professions.

This activity effectively involves students with members of the community who use the language on a daily basis in their professions. Learners also apply skills from the writing process and the technology of desktop publishing to the project. In addition, because the students share their product with their peers, there is an audience other than the teacher. This is a crucial element in motivating students to use the language correctly. The activity could be extended by publishing the newspaper on a regular basis and involving the students from other Spanish classes by having them submit letters to the editor and questions to the "Querida Carmen" column.

PEN PALS AND "EPALS"

In classrooms in two districts located on opposite sides of the country, sixth graders exchange email correspondence with one another in Spanish. Their teachers have facilitated the communication, and once a week the students exchange information on various topics with their pals across the continent. They discuss their families, hobbies and interests, school life, and plans for the upcoming vacation. Some trade photos and brochures from their community for use in a social studies project.

TARGETED STANDARDS	REFLECTION
C Interpersonal Communication	Students describe people and things in their environment and ask questions to obtain information; students write informal messages to each other.

The importance of this activity is that students are seeing a relevant and immediate application of their language learning. Students are motivated to find out how their peers across the country are dealing with the same issues they are. This activity can be expanded to involve students in the target language country.

PRE-ROMAN ITALY

Students in the Italian V class of T.R. Proctor Senior High School make a comparative study of the life and culture of pre-Roman Italy, concentrating on the creations and contributions of the Greek colonies of southern Italy and the Etruscan communities of central Italy. Research and discussion include daily life, towns, religion, and the arts. Students make particular note of the contributions of these cultures that are still seen and used today (i.e., Etruscan arch and funerary art, Greek architecture, city planning, and theater). Students extrapolate information on the lives of the Etruscans by studying their tomb frescoes. In small groups, students then create a series of frescoes depicting the "life journey" of a modern person. Each group then tries to interpret the work of the other groups as if the frescoes were unearthed in the year 4000. After studying some of the Greek myths and legends that take place in Italy, students create classical theater masks for a videotaped dramatization of the legend of Ulysses and the Cyclops.

TARGETED STANDARDS	REFLECTION
Interpersonal Communication	Students use language to discuss their findings of pre-Roman life; they work in groups to produce the murals and the play.
Interpretive Communication	Students read and interpret the messages of a pictorial history (mural) and the moral of a classical myth.
Presentational Communication	Students perform a dramatization.
Relating Cultural Practices to Perspectives	Students learn about the development of artistic and theatrical traditions in western culture.
Relating Cultural Products to Perspectives	Students identify elements of pre-Roman architecture, sculpture, theater, city planning, etc.
Making Connections	Students make connections to disciplines of social studies, history, and the arts.
Acquiring Information and Diverse Perspectives	Students extrapolate the causes for the results of the evolution of Italian culture from its ancient roots.
Language Comparisons	Students develop the ability to express conjecture by the use of grammatical formulas peculiar to Italian, as well as revisit corresponding structures in English.
Cultural Comparisons	Students discuss the artistic and social dynamics of cultures.
Lifelong Learning	By developing a knowledge of fundamental concepts in art, architecture, drama, and social structure, students will better understand and appreciate new encounters in those areas.

This scenario touches upon the Standards in all five of the goal areas. Activities are adaptable to various levels. The unit lends itself to cooperative, aesthetic, and interdisciplinary approaches. Similar scenarios could be designed on a variety of topics that are of particular interest to students or in which the teacher has a particular specialization.

PUERTO RICO, HERE WE COME!

In order to acquaint students with the culture of the language they are learning, kindergarteners in Rockbridge Elementary School's FLEX (Foreign Language Experience) program learn about the culture of Puerto Rico and the traditional dishes that are eaten in this culture. A map and pictures of the island give the students a better view of its location, but original music, traditional dress, traditional food, and authentic musical instruments are still missing. In order to become familiar with these cultural aspects, the students decide to "take a trip" to the island of Puerto Rico in the form of an extended role play. The sound of an airplane departing and arriving is used to make this activity more exciting. After they "arrive" on the island, they listen to taped, authentic music. Using pictures and photographs, they take a trip around the island looking at various things, including traditional homes and dress. Students listen to the vocabulary and repeat it after the teacher. After they "travel" and have fun going from place to place, they are hungry. What better way of ending this activity than eating a traditional dish from the island: *arroz con pollo y habichuelas.*

TARGETED STANDARDS	REFLECTION
Interpersonal Communication	Students learn pertinent vocabulary and ask and answer simple questions about Puerto Rico.
Relating Cultural Products to Perspectives	Students see, hear, and sample various products of the culture studied.

This activity exemplifies the rich experiences that can be provided in a FLEX class. The students are actively involved in learning about the culture in a hands-on experience. The language is introduced as it relates to the cultural topics. A variety of modalities and senses are used so that students are able to "experience" the culture. This activity may be adapted for any grade level or language program model.

RESEARCH PORTFOLIO

Second year students complete an in-depth study of a Spanish-speaking country in this hemisphere in a multi-step process during the semester. In the school media center, the high school students are introduced to the "Countries of the World" program and *DC Newsbank.* Some of the reference sources are available in Spanish. The students produce a portfolio with the following components: a travel brochure describing the country they select; an article in Spanish from the media resources, as well as three pictures, maps and/or drawings; a biography of a famous person from the country; the recipe of a national dish; a song (performed and recorded as audio or video); and an item of the student's choice related to the environment, economics, or politics. The portfolios are kept in the classroom for later use as reference.

TARGETED STANDARDS	REFLECTION
Interpretive Communication	Students read the information researched.
Presentational Communication	Students prepare materials for inclusion in the portfolio.
Acquiring Information and Diverse Perspectives	Students acquire information from authentic documents.
Lifelong Learning	Students consult resources to obtain information on a topic of interest.

This activity demonstrates to students how to access information from the community on a topic of interest. Technology applications are made during this process as students make selections for inclusion in the portfolio. Students are guided through the process, but are also allowed to select an item related to their own interest. The fact that the portfolio will remain in the classroom as a resource for other students makes this activity highly motivating and relevant for the students. The teacher could include peer editing in the process in order to improve the level of accuracy in the materials developed.

RITES OF PASSAGE

The students in Señora Juarez's seventh grade Spanish class have been discussing the traditions in Spanish-speaking countries for identifying when one enters "adulthood." They have been comparing and contrasting ceremonies and rituals, such as the "*los quince años*" with "Sweet Sixteen" parties in the United States. They have also discussed first communions and other religious coming-of-age celebrations. They have made a chart of specific rights and responsibilities that are granted at certain ages in the United States, such as getting a driver's license and being able to vote. Since these students have been learning Spanish since the second grade, they have an extensive vocabulary and are able to communicate on a wide variety of topics relating to their personal interests and needs. From this background, they develop a questionnaire regarding these rites of passage and are assigned to survey at least five members of the Spanish-speaking community and five members of other ethnic backgrounds. Working in groups, they collect and analyze the responses and make summary statements regarding the traditions about one's passage to adulthood in American culture and in the Spanish-speaking world.

TARGETED STANDARDS	REFLECTION
Interpersonal Communication	Students discuss the topic of coming of age.
Interpretive Communication	Students comprehend significant details from their interviews.
Relating Cultural Practices to Perspectives	Students learn how the other country views coming of age.
Cultural Comparisons	Students analyze societal rites of passage in their own culture and in the culture studied.
School and Global Communities	Students use the language in the school and in the local community.

Using geography textbooks from the culture studied, students could research how cultures in various parts of the world mark the coming of age. In some instances they might participate in celebrations which occur in these cultures or reenact some of the celebrations themselves. Participating in a celebration outside of school would add a focus on the Lifelong Learning Standard. Reenacting such a celebration would provide the opportunity to target the Presentational Communication Standard. Other topics that might be addressed in this manner include marriage and death rituals.

THE ROMAN FAMILY

When Ms. Bauer presents the Roman family in her first-year Latin class, the students practice simple sentences aloud and answer questions in Latin regarding the members of the family, what they are wearing, and what they are doing in the picture. This leads to a discussion of the role of each family member in ancient Rome: the father as head of the household; the mother as the primary teacher of the daughter, who marries around the age of 12; and the son as the student who learns to conduct business as his father does. Ms. Bauer then asks the students to discuss how the family roles in American culture are different and some of the reasons for these differences. Students who have a background in other cultures are encouraged to discuss the roles of family members of their culture. Ms. Bauer then introduces the students to a passage in Latin that discusses the Roman family, which the students are easily able to comprehend because of the prior oral and visual preparation. Finally, Ms. Bauer asks students to summarize what they noticed in the story with regard to adjectives that describe, respectively, female and male members of the family. Students describe what they noticed in the passage and how this relates to noun/adjective agreement and gender in the English language.

TARGETED STANDARDS	REFLECTION
Interpersonal Communication	Students use Latin to ask and answer questions.
Interpretive Communication	Students read and understand the Latin passage.
Relating Cultural Practices to Perspectives	Students understand the organization and the roles of the Roman family.
Relating Cultural Products to Perspectives	Students understand the setting of the Roman house and some Roman clothing.
Language Comparisons	Students understand the concept of noun/adjective agreement and gender and how it compares to the English language.
Cultural Comparisons	Students recognize the similarities and differences found in the concept of family and how this concept relates to that of American and other cultures.

The discussion of the family is relevant to all languages and could also be focused on a myriad of topics. The first-year class would be appropriate for elementary, middle school, or high school students. Relating this discussion to information from history or social studies (either from an earlier year, or currently) would help move the scenario into a focus on the Making Connections Standard. The language system as a curricular element plays a role in helping students understand the Latin syntax and compare it with English. If the class included students who spoke a Romance language at home, a third comparison could be made. These students already control adjective agreement in their first language and find the Latin not to be a problem. The use of Latin orally while using visuals helps students internalize language structures, which facilitates their comprehension of the Latin passage.

ROMAN MARRIAGE

In Mr. Burgess's first year Latin class, the students are planning a re-creation of an authentic Roman wedding. Each of the Brockwood High School students receives a handout from their teacher about Roman marriage. The handout includes the marriage contract, the sequence of events, and the script the participants will read during the ceremony, along with pertinent vocabulary in Latin. After discussing the handout, the students choose roles. There will be a bride and a groom, priest, augur, and many other Romans. All of the students who do not have a specific role will participate in the procession to the groom's house. After they have enacted the ceremony in Latin, they discuss information in the handout and compare Roman weddings with weddings in American culture.

TARGETED STANDARDS	REFLECTION
Presentational Communication	Students participate in the ceremony using Latin.
Relating Cultural Products to Perspectives	Students participate in the reenactment of a ceremony from the culture studied.
Cultural Comparisons	Students discuss differences in the historical re-creation and practices in today's society.

An extension of this activity could include searching the Internet for literary works of Latin authors for references to Roman marriages by using the vocabulary learned to search for appropriate passages. Students could be asked to compare the marriage customs through the centuries as presented by various authors during different literary periods. To bring in the language system, the teacher might ask students to identify specific syntax that is found in the marriage ceremony and how this reflects the attitude of the Romans toward marriage and the role of bride and groom in the ceremony.

RUSSIAN SCIENCE PROJECT

Students at Captain Nathan Hale Middle School begin a pen pal correspondence on the Internet with a school in Moscow. Over the years, this leads to an exchange of students, teachers, and community members between the U.S. and Russian communities. A Russian teacher reads about the exchange in the local newpaper and volunteers to teach students Russian. Since the students are involved in a science project on rocketry with their Russian counterparts, the first words they learn are Russian space terms and how to count backwards from 10 for lift-off. They build model rockets and launch them in their own communities in Russia and in the United States. The students use computer software to develop stacks of pictures and words in English and Russian, along with the pronunciation and Russian background music. Russian language instruction is now an integral part of the curriculum at Nathan Hale Middle School.

TARGETED STANDARDS	REFLECTION
C Interpersonal Communication	Students use written language to communicate with their Russian peers via the Internet.
C Making Connections	Students acquire information about science in the target language.
C School and Global Communities	Students communicate orally and in writing with members of the other culture regarding topics of personal interest, community, or world concern.

This scenario illustrates how a purposeful learning activity with students in another country can motivate students to learn the language and influence world language offerings in the school. The focus of the language instruction is also driven by the science topic that the students are currently studying, providing an excellent example of making connections across disciplines.

FREQUENTLY ASKED QUESTIONS

What is the relationship of the World-Readiness Standards to states and local districts?

The World-Readiness Standards are intended to serve as a gauge for excellence as states and local districts carry out their responsibilities for curriculum in the schools. The political context requires that national standards be voluntary and that they do not usurp the role of the states. The National Standards are neither curriculum nor are they substitutes for state frameworks; that is why they do not reflect a level of detail that teachers are accustomed to seeing in local documents. The World-Readiness Standards provide a consistent vision of the five broad goals for learning world languages (the Five Cs). These five goals are intentionally broad to accommodate the wide variety of program models for learning world languages, pre-K through adult, found across the United States. These broad goal statements allow states and districts to further define the Standards according to their individual program models. It is important to remember that all world language programs, regardless of model, must consistently integrate the 5 Cs in order to meet the overarching goals for learning world languages.

How do the World-Readiness Standards relate to the ACTFL Proficiency Guidelines?

The World-Readiness Standards include five Goal Areas (the 5 Cs) along with their 11 associated standards (see page 9). They encompass purposes for learning world languages that go beyond linguistic skills. The ACTFL Proficiency Guidelines describe the four skills of Listening, Reading, Speaking, and Writing. They "present the levels of proficiency as ranges, and describe what an individual can and cannot do with language at each level, regardless of where, when, or how the language was acquired." (ACTFL Proficiency Guidelines 2012, p. 3). In order to have a deeper understanding of the Communication standard, it is useful for teachers and learners to become familiar with the descriptions of the levels of proficiency found in the Proficiency Guidelines. Educators and learners use this understanding to improve learners' language performance, focusing on what it takes to move to the next level.

Are the World-Readiness Standards mandatory?

The World-Readiness Standards are voluntary. They identify the key instructional goal areas for world language programs (the 5 Cs), and the 11 standards that further define the five goal areas. The Standards guide state and local policy makers, curriculum developers, and instructors in making decisions about the content of high quality world language programs.

Why does this document specify that world languages are for <u>all</u> learners?

Identifying the refreshed Standards for Foreign Language Learning as **World-Readiness** Standards for Learning Languages communicates that learning languages is critical for all learners in order to be prepared for today's world where "global" is a term used to describe almost everything from products to customers. Whether a learner pursues a career in international business or works for a locally owned company, the opportunities to do business with and to communicate with people from different cultural and linguistic backgrounds are steadily increasing. More and more people are realizing the practical application of speaking more than one language in all areas of the workforce as well as in daily interactions in the community. The following workplaces identified increasing needs for employees with communication skills in more than one language: health care, education, customer service, hospitality, government, finance, information technology, social services, and law enforcement (Lee, 2012). Add to this the fact that the average worker today stays at each of his or her jobs for 4.4 years, according to the Bureau of Labor Statistics (2014). To be world-ready, all learners need knowledge and skills in what Michael Byram calls "intercultural communicative competence" (Byram, 1997).

Is instructional time divided equally among all 5 Cs?

The 5 Cs are interconnected; together, they represent learning goals present in every unit of instruction. Communication and Cultures are inextricably linked in daily instruction. Connections, Comparisons, and Communities support Communication and Cultures, providing purpose and context for intercultural communicative competence. The goal areas (5 Cs) and the associated Standards represent the consensus of the field as to the overall objectives of second language learning.

What if I only have time for the Communication goal?

The Communication goal is indeed important but it cannot be taught in isolation. To be world-ready, learners need to be able to understand cultures, to respond in culturally appropriate ways, to access information from a variety of authentic sources, to gain insight into their own language and culture, to collaborate with others virtually, and to share and apply what they have learned beyond the school setting. The Cultures, Connections, Comparisons, and Communities goal areas provide content, context, and purpose for Communication.

What is the role of grammar?

The Standards along with the Proficiency Guidelines emphasize meaningful and purposeful use of the target language in situations where there is a real need to communicate. Grammar is not the goal of instruction in world language programs but, instead, a tool that learners use to communicate clearly. It is important that learners experience multiple examples of a grammatical structure in meaningful contexts. Adair-Hauck and Donato (2002) suggest that the teacher use these examples to guide learners through a series of tasks that allow the learners to discover the grammatical rule highlighted in the examples.

How do I use the Standards if our district does not have a K–12 program in world languages?

The Standards document describes the content goals for all world language programs, independent of length of sequence or entry or exit points. Curriculum planners can use the Standards document to guide the choice of content required for high quality language learning experiences. In addition, the document provides sample performance indicators for Novice, Intermediate, and Advanced levels. Figure 4 shows expected levels of performance that learners can achieve in programs of various lengths. Note that learners achieve the Advanced Level in programs that begin in early elementary grades and provide continuous standards-based learning through the end of high school and beyond. At the state and local level, curriculum planners can use the Standards document as a tool for planning present programs and as a powerful description of what could be accomplished if resources and time could be provided for extended sequences of language study.

Figure 4. Time As a Critical Component for Developing Language Performance

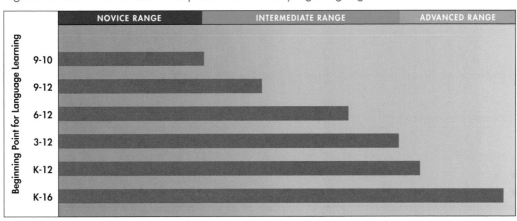

From the *Performance Descriptors for Language Learners* (ACTFL, 2012a, p. 13)

How do we articulate with a standards-based program?

A major articulation issue is the placement of students who have participated in a standards-based program using assessment instruments that measure vocabulary and grammar but do not measure what they know and are able to do with the language. States, districts, schools, universities, and organizations provide a variety of instruments for placing learners in a next level of instruction. Programs still need assessments of performance which provide evidence of how well learners use the language in meeting the Standards.

Are literacy and 21st century skills part of the Standards?

In the recent revision of the Standards, input and feedback affirmed that literacy and 21st century skills needed to be embedded in the Standards. In the description for each goal area, educators will notice the active application of language skills for real-world purposes. Specific words were added in the refreshed Standards in order to emphasize both literacy and 21st century skills, such as communication and collaboration, creativity, and critical thinking and problem solving. This is an important update to focus language learning and connect with needs of learners in pre-kindergarten through graduate school and those already in careers. The World-Readiness Standards for Learning Languages connect language learning with literacy and 21st century skills.

APPENDIXES

REFERENCES

Adair-Hauck, B. & Donato, R. (2002). The PACE model : A story-based approach to meaning and form for standards-based language learning. *The French Review. 76*, 265-296.

American Council on the Teaching of Foreign Languages (ACTFL). (1986). *ACTFL proficiency guidelines.* Hastings-on-Hudson, NY: Author.

American Council on the Teaching of Foreign Languages (ACTFL). (2012a). *ACTFL performance descriptors for language learners.* Alexandria, VA: Author.

American Council on the Teaching of Foreign Languages (ACTFL). (2012b). *Position statement on the use of the target language in the classroom.* Retrieved from http://www.actfl.org/news/position-statements/use-the-target-language-the-classroom

American Council on the Teaching of Foreign Languages (ACTFL). (2012c). *ACTFL proficiency guidelines.* Alexandria, VA: Author.

American Council on the Teaching of Foreign Languages (ACTFL). (2014). *Position statement on global competence.* Alexandria, VA: Author. Retrieved from http://www.actfl.org/news/position-statements/global-competence-position-statement

Bachman, L. F. (1990). *Fundamental considerations in language testing.* Oxford: Oxford University Press.

Bialystok, E. (1981). The role of linguistic knowledge in second language use. *Studies in Second Language Learning, 1,* 1–45.

Bialystok, E. (1999). Cognitive complexity and attentional control in the bilingual mind. *Child Development, 70*(3), 636–644.

Bialystok, E. (2005). *Consequences of bilingualism for cognitive development.* New York: Oxford University Press.

Bialystok, E., Peets, K.F. & Moreno, S. (2014). Producing bilinguals through immersion education : Development of metalinguistic awareness. *Applied Psycholinguistics, 35*(1), 177-191

Brecht, R. D., & Walton, A. R. (1994). The future shape of language learning in the new world of global communication: Consequences for higher education and beyond. In R. Donato & R.M. Terry (Eds.), *Foreign language learning: The journey of a lifetime.* Lincolnwood, IL: National Textbook Co.

Bureau of Labor Statistics. (2014). Employee Tenure Summary. *Economic News Release.* USDL-14-1714. Retrieved from http://www.bls.gov/news.release/tenure.nr0.htm

Byram, M. (1997). *Teaching and assessing intercultural communicative competence.* Clevedon, UK: Multilingual Matters.

Cade, J. M. (1997). The foreign language immersion program in the Kansas City, Missouri Public Schools, 1986–1996 [Abstract]. *Dissertation Abstracts International A, 58*(10), 3838.

Canale, M., & Swain, M. (1980). Theoretical bases of communicative approaches to second language teaching and testing. *Applied Linguistics, 1,* 1–47.

Cooper, T. C., Yanosky, D. J., Wisenbaker, J. M., Jahner, D., Webb, E., & Wilbur, M. L. (2008). Foreign language learning and SAT verbal scores revisited. *Foreign Language Annals, 41*(2), 200–217.

Council of Europe. (2001). *Common European framework of reference for languages: Learning, teaching, assessment.* Strasbourg, France: Cambridge University Press.

Curtain, H. A. & Dahlberg, C. A. (2010). Languages and children, making the match: New languages for young learners (4th ed.). Boston: Pearson.

de Jong, J. H. A. L., & Verhoeven, L. (1992). Modeling and assessing language proficiency. In L. Verhoeven & J.H.A.L. de Jong (Eds.), *The construct of language proficiency.* Amsterdam: John Benjamins.

Fromkin, V. & Rodman, R. (1993). *An introduction to language.* New York: Holt, Rinehart, and Winston.

Hymes, D. (1985). Toward linguistic competence. *Revue d l'AILA: AILA Review, 2,* 9–23.

Lee, J. (2012, November 26). Bilingual jobs : Foreign-language careers on rise. *Chicago Tribune.* Retrieved from http://articles.chicagotribune.com/2012-11-26/classified/chi-bilingual-jobs-20121126_1_foreign-language-foreign-language-fastest-growing-language

Magnan, S., Murphy, D., Sahakyan, N., & Kim, S. (2012). Student goals, expectations, and the standards for foreign language learning. *Foreign Language Annals, 45*(2), 170–192.

Mårtensson, J., Eriksson,J., Bodammer, N.C., Lindgren, M., Johansson, M., Nyberg, L., & Lövdén, M. (2012). Growth of language-related brain areas after foreign language learning. *NeuroImage, 63*(1), 240-244

Modern Language Association. (2007). *Foreign languages and higher education: New structures for a changed world.* New York: Author.

Museums, Libraries, and 21st Century Skills. (n.d.). *Visual literacy.* Retrieved from http://www.imls.gov/about/21st_century_skills_list.aspx

National Art Education Association. (1995). *Visual arts education reform handbook.* Reston, VA: Author.

National Council of State Supervisors for Languages (NCSSFL). (2010). *LinguaFolio training modules; 5.2. What is interculturality?* Retrieved from http://www.learnnc.org/lp/editions/linguafolio/6122

National Council of State Supervisors for Languages (NCSSFL) & American Council on the Teaching of Foreign Languages (ACTFL). (2013). *NCSSFL-ACTFL can-do statements.* Alexandria, VA: ACTFL.

Phillips, J. & Abbott, M. (2011). *A decade of foreign language standards: Influence, impact, and future directions.* Alexandria, VA: ACTFL.

Rhodes, N. & Pufahl, I. (2010). *Foreign language teaching in U.S. schools: Results of a national survey.* Washington, DC: Center for Applied Linguistics.

Savignon, S. J. (1983). *Communicative competence: Theory and classroom practice.* Menlo Park, CA: Addison-Wesley Publishing Company.

Schiffrin, D. (1994). *Approaches to discourse.* Oxford: Blackwell.

RESOURCES

Database of publications on the National Standards: http://www.actfl.org/standards/database

Annenberg Learner: Teacher Resources/Foreign Language. Teaching foreign languages K–12: A library of classroom practices (video library, guide, and resources). http://learner.org/resources/series185.html

Center for Advanced Research on Language Acquisition (CARLA). http://www.carla.umn.edu/

Arens, K. (2008). Genres and the standards: Teaching the 5 C's through texts. *German Quarterly, 81*(1), 35-48.

Byrnes, H. (2008). Articulating a foreign language sequence through content: A look at the culture standards. *Language Teaching, 41*(1), 103-118.

Clementi, D. & Terrill, L. (2013). *The keys to planning for learning: Effective curriculum, unit, and lesson design.* Alexandria, VA: American Council on the Teaching of Foreign Languages.

Everson, M. E. (2009). The importance of standards. In M. E. Everson & Y. Xiao (Ed.), *Teaching Chinese as a foreign language: Theories and applications* (pp. 3-17). Boston, MA: Cheng &Tsui.

Fantini, A. E. (1999). Comparisons: Towards the development of intercultural competence. In J. K. Phillips (Ed.), *Foreign language standards: Linking research, theories, and practices* (pp. 165-218). Lincolnwood, IL: National Textbook Company.

Galloway, V. (Ed.). (2001). *Teaching cultures of the Hispanic world: Products and practices in perspective.* AATSP professional development series handbook for teachers K–16, Volume IV. Mason, OH: Thomson Learning

Hall, J. K. (2002). *Methods for teaching foreign languages: Creating a community of learners in the classroom.* Upper Saddle River, NJ: Prentice Hall.

Jensen, J. (2007). National foreign language policy: A state language coordinator's perspective. *Modern Language Journal, 91*(2), 261-264.

Kern, R. (2008). Making connections through texts in language teaching. *Language Teaching, 41*(3), 367-387.

Lange, D. L. (2003). Future directions for culture teaching and learning: Implications of the new culture standards and theoretical frameworks for curriculum, assessment, instruction, and research. In D. L. Lange & R. M Paige (Eds.), *Culture as the core: Perspectives on culture in second language learning* (pp. 337-353). Greenwich, CT: Information Age Publishing.

Larson, P. (2006). The return of the text: A welcome challenge for less commonly taught languages. *Modern Language Journal, 90*(2), 255-258.

Long, D. R. (1999). Breaking down the barriers: Implications of standards for foreign language learning for United States universities. *ADFL Bulletin, 31*(1), 78-79.

Magnan, S. M., Murphy, D, and Sahakyan, N. (2014). Goals of collegiate learners and the standards for foreign language learning. Supplement Issue: Monograph Issue. In B.A. Lafford (Ed.). *Modern Language Journal, 98*(S1).

Phillips, J. K. & Terry, R. M. (Eds.). (1999). *Foreign language standards: Linking research, theories, and practices.* Lincolnwood, IL: National Textbook Company.

Potowski, K., Berne, J., Clark, A. & Hammerand, A. (2008). Spanish for K–8 heritage speakers: A standards-based curriculum project. *Hispania, 91*(1), 25-41.

Scott, V. M. (Ed.). (2009). *Principles and practices of the standards in college foreign Language education.* Boston, MA: Heinle.

Shrum, J. L. & Glisan, E. W. (2010). *Teacher's handbook: Contextualized language instruction.* (4th ed.) Boston, MA: Heinle.

Valdés, G. (1995). The teaching of minority languages as "foreign" languages: Pedagogical and theoretical challenges. *Modern Language Journal, 79*(3), 299-328.

INTERPRETIVE MODE: PERFORMANCE DESCRIPTORS

The Performance Descriptors outline the range of performance that learners exhibit in the Interpretive Mode of Communication, highlighting strategies that learners should use as they construct meaning through reading, listening to, or viewing authentic materials. Second language learners use a variety of strategies acquired in their first language to construct meaning in the second language. Improving performance in the Interpretive Mode is not just about accessing more complex texts, rather it is through consciously using a wider variety of strategies to understand what is heard, read, or viewed, including top-down strategies (using background knowledge and context clues to figure out the meaning) as well as bottom-up strategies (discriminating between sounds and letters or recognizing characters, recognizing word-order patterns, analyzing sentence structure, examining parts of words to try to decipher meaning). In learners' first language, phonics work because they have a bank of oral language that they can convert to written. In learners' second language, educators need to first activate top-down strategies so learners understand the overall meaning and context before using bottom-up strategies to refine their initial understanding. To strengthen learners' performance in the Interpretive Mode, instructors should provide ample access to authentic materials. These Performance Descriptors and Performance Indicators are intended to show the range of receptive skills that learners should practice at all levels of instruction.

Performance Descriptors: Interpretive Mode

NOVICE RANGE
Understands words, phrases, and formulaic language that have been practiced and memorized to get meaning of the main idea from simple, highly predictable oral or written texts with strong visual support.
INTERMEDIATE RANGE
Understands main ideas and some supporting details on familiar topics from a variety of texts.
ADVANCED RANGE
Understands main ideas and supporting details on familiar and some new concrete topics from a variety of more complex texts that have a clear, organized structure.

NCSSFL-ACTFL Can-Do Statements

Interpretive Mode – Listening

GLOBAL STATEMENT	SAMPLE INDICATORS
NOVICE RANGE – INTERPRETIVE LISTENING	
Novice Low Learners can recognize a few memorized words and phrases when they hear them spoken.	**Novice Low Learners can** <ul><li>occasionally identify the sound of a character or a word</li><li>occasionally understand isolated words that they have memorized, particularly when accompanied by gestures or pictures</li></ul>

continued

GLOBAL STATEMENT	SAMPLE INDICATORS
Novice Mid Learners can recognize some familiar words and phrases when they hear them spoken.	**Novice Mid Learners can** • understand a few courtesy phrases • recognize and sometimes understand basic information in words and phrases that they have memorized • recognize and sometimes understand words and phrases that they have learned for specific purposes
Novice High Learners can often understand words, phrases, and simple sentences related to everyday life. They can recognize pieces of information and sometimes understand the main topic of what is being said.	**Novice High Learners can** • sometimes understand simple questions or statements on familiar topics • understand simple information when presented with pictures and graphs • sometimes understand the main topic of conversations that they overhear
INTERMEDIATE RANGE – INTERPRETIVE LISTENING	
Intermediate Low Learners can understand the main idea in short, simple messages and presentations on familiar topics. They can understand the main idea of simple conversations that they overhear.	**Intermediate Low Learners can** • understand the basic purpose of a message • understand messages related to their basic needs • understand questions and simple statements on everyday topics when they are part of the conversation
Intermediate Mid Learners can understand the main idea in messages and presentations on a variety of topics related to everyday life and personal interests and studies. They can understand the main idea in conversations that they overhear.	**Intermediate Mid Learners can** • understand basic information in ads, announcements, and other simple recordings • understand the main idea of what they listen to for personal enjoyment • understand messages related to their everyday life
Intermediate High Learners can easily understand the main idea in messages and presentations on a variety of topics related to everyday life and personal interests and studies. They can usually understand a few details of what they overhear in conversations, even when something unexpected is expressed. They can sometimes follow what they hear about events and experiences in various time frames.	**Intermediate High Learners can** • easily understand straightforward information or interactions • understand a few details in ads, announcements, and other simple recordings • sometimes understand situations with complicating factors
ADVANCED RANGE – INTERPRETIVE LISTENING	
Advanced Low Learners can understand the main idea and some supporting details in organized speech on a variety of topics of personal and general interest. They can follow stories and descriptions of some length and in various time frames. They can understand information presented in a variety of genres on familiar topics, even when something unexpected is expressed.	**Advanced Low Learners can** • understand descriptions and stories of events that have happened or will happen • understand the main idea of popular genres

continued

GLOBAL STATEMENT	SAMPLE INDICATORS
Advanced Mid Learners can understand the main idea and most supporting details on a variety of topics of personal and general interest, as well as some topics of professional interest. They can follow stories and descriptions of some length and in various time frames. They can understand information presented in most genres, even when not familiar with the topic.	**Advanced Mid Learners can** • understand the main idea and many details of descriptions or interviews • understand accounts of events • understand directions and instructions on everyday tasks
Advanced High Learners can easily follow narrative, informational, and descriptive speech. They can understand discussions on most topics that deal with special interests, unfamiliar situations, and abstract concepts. They can sometimes follow extended arguments and different points of view.	**Advanced High Learners can** • easily understand detailed reports and exposés • often understand various viewpoints in extended arguments • understand discussions and presentations on many concrete and abstract topics
SUPERIOR RANGE – INTERPRETIVE LISTENING	
Superior Learners can follow a wide range of academic and professional discourse on abstract and specialized topics. They can understand all standard dialects. They can sometimes infer complex meaning that requires deep understanding of the culture.	**Superior Learners can** • understand a variety of abstract and technical topics within their field of expertise • understand discussions on various issues of general interest • understand implications and inferences in discussions or presentations

Interpretive Mode – Reading

GLOBAL STATEMENT	SAMPLE INDICATORS
NOVICE RANGE – INTERPRETIVE READING	
Novice Low Learners can recognize a few letters or characters. They can identify a few memorized words and phrases when they read.	**Novice Low Learners can** • recognize a few letters or characters • connect some words, phrases, or characters to their meanings
Novice Mid Learners can recognize some letters or characters. They can understand some learned or memorized words and phrases when they read.	**Novice Mid Learners can** • recognize words, phrases, and characters with the help of visuals • recognize words, phrases, and characters when they associate them with things they already know
Novice High Learners can understand familiar words, phrases, and sentences within short and simple texts related to everyday life. They can sometimes understand the main idea of what they have read.	**Novice High Learners can** • usually understand short simple messages on familiar topics • sometimes understand short simple descriptions with the help of pictures or graphs • sometimes understand the main idea of published materials • understand simple everyday notices in public places on topics that are familiar to them

continued

GLOBAL STATEMENT	SAMPLE INDICATORS
INTERMEDIATE RANGE – INTERPRETIVE READING	
Intermediate Low Learners can understand the main idea of short and simple texts when the topic is familiar.	**Intermediate Low Learners can** • understand messages in which the writer tells or asks them about topics of personal interest • identify some simple information needed on forms • identify some information from news media
Intermediate Mid Learners can understand the main idea of texts related to everyday life and personal interests or studies.	**Intermediate Mid Learners can** • understand simple personal questions • understand basic information in ads, announcements, and other simple texts • understand the main idea of what they read for personal enjoyment • read simple written exchanges between other people
Intermediate High Learners can easily understand the main idea of texts related to everyday life, personal interests, and studies. They can sometimes follow stories and descriptions about events and experiences in various time frames.	**Intermediate High Learners can** • understand accounts of personal events or experiences • sometimes follow short, written instructions when supported by visuals • understand the main idea of and a few supporting facts about famous people and historic events
ADVANCED RANGE – INTERPRETIVE READING	
Advanced Low Learners can understand the main idea and some supporting details on a variety of topics of personal and general interest. They can follow stories and descriptions of some length and in various time frames and genres.	**Advanced Low Learners can** • find and use information for practical purposes • read texts that compare and contrast information • follow simple written instructions
Advanced Mid Learners can understand the main idea and most supporting details in texts on a variety of topics of personal and general interest, as well as some professional topics. They can follow stories and descriptions of considerable length and in various time frames. They can understand texts written in a variety of genres, even when they are unfamiliar with the topic.	**Advanced Mid Learners can** • follow the general idea and some details of what is written in a variety of stories and autobiographical accounts • understand general information on topics outside their field of interest • understand messages on a wide variety of past, present, and future events
Advanced High Learners can easily follow narrative, informational, and descriptive texts. They can understand what they read on most topics that deal with special interests, unfamiliar situations, and abstract concepts. They can sometimes understand extended arguments and different points of view.	**Advanced High Learners can** • understand narrative, descriptive, and informational texts of any length • read about most topics of special interest • read most general fiction and non-fiction
SUPERIOR RANGE – INTERPRETIVE READING	
Superior Learners can follow academic, professional, and literary texts on a wide range of both familiar and unfamiliar subjects. They can sometimes infer complex meaning that requires analysis and deep understanding of the culture.	**Superior Learners can** • analyze the primary argument and supporting details • understand detailed information within and beyond their fields of interest • comprehend complex texts on abstract topics of interest to them

PROJECT PERSONNEL

The World-Readiness Standards for Learning Languages were revised from previous editions based on what language educators have learned from more than 15 years of implementing the Standards. The process was overseen and guided by the Standards Collaborative Board, through the representatives of the following national organizations:

American Association of Teachers of Arabic
American Association of Teachers of French
American Association of Teachers of German
American Association of Teachers of Italian
American Association of Teachers of Japanese
American Association of Teachers of Korean
American Association of Teachers of Modern Greek
American Association of Teachers of Spanish and Portuguese
American Classical League
American Council of Teachers of Russian/American Council for Collaboration in Education
    and Language Study
American Council on the Teaching of Foreign Languages
American Sign Language Teachers Association
Chinese Language Association of Secondary-Elementary Schools
Chinese Language Teachers Association
Modern Language Association
National Council of Less Commonly Taught Languages
National Standards Task Force for Hindi

Members of the writing group for the process to refresh the National Standards:

Ann Marie Gunter, North Carolina Department of Public Instruction, Raleigh, NC
Kathryn Hartung, Wauwatosa School District, Wauwatosa, WI
Alisha Dawn Samples, Lexington County School District One, Lexington, SC
Paul Sandrock, ACTFL, Alexandria, VA
Martin Smith, West Windsor-Plainsboro Regional School District, Princeton, NJ
Jacqueline Van Houten, Kentucky Department of Education, Lexington, KY; Jefferson
    County School District, Louisville, KY

Revisions to this generic volume of the National Standards were based on previous editions.

Lead writers
June K. Phillips, Weber State University, Ogden, UT (Retired)
Don Reutershan, Maine Department of Education, August, ME (Retired)

Contributing writers
Anita Alkhas, University of Wisconsin-Milwaukee
Donna Clementi, Lawrence University, Appleton, WI
Kathryn Hartung, Wauwatosa School District, Wauwatosa, WI

PROJECT PERSONNEL FOR THE FIRST EDITION OF THE NATIONAL STANDARDS (1996)

Project Director: June K. Phillips, Weber State University, Ogden, UT

K–12 Student Standards Task Force

Christine Brown (Chair)
Glastonbury Public Schools
Glastonbury, CT

Marty Abbott
Fairfax County Public Schools
Fairfax County, VA

Keith Cothrun
Las Cruces High School
Las Cruces, NM

Beverly Harris-Schenz
University of Pittsburgh
Pittsburgh, PA

Denise Mesa
Sabal Palm Elementary
North Miami Beach, FL

Genelle Morain
University of Georgia
Athens, GA

Marjorie Tussing
California State University
Fullerton, CA

Guadalupe Valdés
Stanford University
Palo Alto, CA

A. Ronald Walton
National Foreign Language
Center
Washington, DC

John Webb
Hunter College High School
New York, NY

Thomas Welch
Jessamine County Public Schools
Nicholasville, KY

TASK FORCE MEMBERS FOR LANGUAGE-SPECIFIC NATIONAL STANDARDS

Standards for Learning American Sign Language (2013)

A Project of the American Sign Language Teachers Association

Task Force on Standards for Learning American Sign Language
Glenna Ashton, (Chair), University of Florida, Gainesville, FL
Keith Cagle, Gallaudet University, Washington, DC
Kim Brown Kurz, National Technical Institute for the Deaf, Rochester, NY
William Newell, Washington School for the Deaf, Vancouver, WA
Rico Peterson, National Technical Institute for the Deaf, Rochester, NY
Jason E. Zinza, University of Maryland, College Park, MD

Standards for Learning Arabic K–16 in the United States (2006)

A collaborative effort of the Arabic K–12 Materials Development Project, the National Capital Language Resource Center, the National Standards Collaborative, the American Association of Teachers of Arabic, and the National Middle East Language Resource Center.

The Task Force on Standards for the Learning of Arabic K–16
Mahdi Alosh (Chair), Ohio State University, Columbus, OH
Nesreen Akhtarkhavari, private consultant, Chicago, IL
Christine Brown, Glastonbury Public Schools, Glastonbury, CT
Ferial Demy, Foreign Service Institute, U.S. Department of State, Washington, DC
Muhammad S. Eissa, Eissa & Associates, Chicago, IL

Shawn Greenstreet, National Capital Language Resource Center, Washington, DC
Iman Arabi-Katbi Hashem, Occidental College, Los Angeles, CA
Wafa Hassan, Islamic Saudi Academy, Alexandria, VA
Dora Johnson, National Capital Language Resource Center, Washington, DC
Lina Kholaki, New Horizon Schools, Los Angeles, CA
Wafaa Makki, Dearborn Public Schools, Dearborn, MI
Kathleen McBroom, Dearborn Public Schools, Dearborn, MI
Khitam Abder-Ruhman Omar, Fairfax Public Schools, Fairfax, VA

Standards for Chinese Language Learning (1999)

A Project of the Chinese Language Association of Secondary-Elementary Schools (CLASS) with the Chinese Language Teachers Association

Task Force Members
Chih-Wen Su (Co-Chair), Amherst Regional Middle/ High School, Amherst, MA
Lucy Lee (Co-Chair), Livingston High School, Livingston, NJ
Carol Shao-Yuan Chen-Lin, Choate Rosemary Hall, Wallingford, CT
Yu-Lan Lin, Boston Public Schools, Boston, MA
Claire Kotenbeutel, James Madison Memorial High School, Madison, WI
Hal Nicolas, Cape Elementary/ Dunbar Middle/ Fort Myers High School, Ft. Myers, FL
Catherine Yen, Abraham Lincoln High School, San Francisco, CA

Regional Committee
Tom Buckingham, Cape Elementary/Trafalgar Middle/Cape Coral High School, Ft. Myers, FL
Floyd Chamberlin, Southport High School, Indianapolis, IN
Xiaoling Chang, Abraham Lincoln High School, San Francisco, CA
Vicky Chin, Lowell High School, San Francisco, CA
Lina Hsieh, Sidwell Friends School, Washington, DC
Caroline Huang, Venice High Schoo, Los Angeles, CA
Dorothy Ong, Lowell High School, San Francisco, CA

Standards for Classical Language Learning (1997)

A Collaborative Project of The American Classical League and The American Philological Association and Regional Classical Associations

Task Force on Standards for Classical Language Learning
Richard C. Gascoyne, University at Albany, SUNY, Albany, NY (Chair)
Martha Abbott, Fairfax County Public Schools, Fairfax, VA
Philip Ambrose, The University of Vermont, Burlington, VT
Cathy Daugherty, The Electronic Classroom, Richmond, VA
Sally Davis, Arlington County Public Schools, Arlington, VA
Terry Klein, North Allegheny School District, Pittsburgh, PA
Glenn Knudsvig, University of Michigan, Ann Arbor, MI
Robert LaBouve, Southwest Educational Development Laboratory, Austin, TX
Nancy Lister, Vernon Public Schools, Vernon, CT
Karen Lee Singh, Florida State University School, Tallahassee, FL

Kathryn A. Thomas, Creighton University, Omaha, NE
Richard F. Thomas, Harvard University, Cambridge, MA

Standards for the Learning of French, K–16 (1999)

AATF Task Force on Standards for the Learning of French
Rebecca M. Valette, Boston College, Chestnut Hill, MA, Co-chair
Margot M. Steinhart, Northwestern University, Evanston, IL, Co-chair
Barbara C. Anderson, Normandale French Immersion School, Edina, MN
Pat Barr-Harrison, Prince George's County Schools, Capitol Heights, MD
Assia Bérubé, Good Counsel High School, Chicago, IL
N. Patricia R. Duggar, Paul Breaux Middle School, Lafayette, LA
Eveline Leisner, Los Angeles Valley College, Van Nuys, CA
Joyce P. Lentz, Las Cruces High School, Las Cruces, NM
Janel Lafond Paquin, Rogers High School, Newport, RI
Alain Ranwez, Metropolitan State College, Denver, CO
Flore Zéphir, University of Missouri, Columbia, MO

Standards for Learning German (1999)

A Project of the American Association of Teachers of German

K–16 Student Standards Task Force
Marjorie Tussing (Co-Chair), California State University-Fullerton, CA
Susan Webber (Co-Chair), Meadowdale Sr. High School, Lynnwood, WA
Liette Bohler, Tidewater Community College, Virginia Beach, VA
Thomas Keith Cothrun, Las Cruces High School, Las Cruces, NM
Carol Ann Pesola Dahlberg, Concordia College, Moorhead, MN
Paul A. García, School District of Kansas City, MO (Retired)
Margaret Hampton, Earlham College, Richmond, IN
Carl H. Johnson, Texas Education Agency, Austin, TX
Zoe E. Louton, Educational Service Unit #5, Beatrice, NE
Karl F. Otto, Jr., University of Pennsylvania, Philadelphia, PA
Jim Sheppard, Screven County High School, Sylvania, GA
Helene Zimmer-Loew, American Association of Teachers of German, Cherry Hill, NJ

Standards for Learning Hindi: Novice to Superior Levels (2014)

National Standards Task Force for Hindi
Vijay Gambhir (Project Director & Chair), University of Pennsylvania, Philadelphia, PA
Susham Bedi (Co-Chair), Columbia University, NY
Madhu Aggarwal, Madhu Bhasha Kendra Language Center, Fremont, CA
Surendra Gambhir, University of Pennsylvania, Philadelphia, PA
Seema Khurana, Yale University, CT
Gyanam Mahajan, University of California, Los Angeles, CA
Madhu Maheshwari, India International School, Annandale, VA
Arun Prakash, Bellaire High School, Houston, TX; University of Houston, TX

Gautami Shah, University of Texas at Austin, TX

Kiron Sharma, Farleigh Dickinson University, NJ; Vidyalaya (School of Indian Languages & Culture), Parsippany, NJ

Anchala Sobrin, John Jay High School, NY; Hudson Valley Hindi School, NY

Herman van Olphen, University of Texas at Austin, TX; Hindi Urdu Flagship Program at the University of Texas at Austin, TX

Standards for Learning Italian (2006)

National Standards Task Force of the American Association of Teachers of Italian

Dr. Grace Mannino (Co-Chair), Brentwood High School, Brentwood, NY; SUNY at Stonybrook; and Suffolk Community College, Selden, NY

Ida Giampietro Wilder (Co-Chair), Greece Athena High School and Nazareth College, Rochester, NY

Rosa Bellino-Giordano, Lyons Township High School, LaGrange, IL

Mario Donatelli, Ramapo High School, Spring Valley, NY

Bruna Furgiuele, East Rochester Middle School, East Rochester, NY

Lucrezia Lindia, Eastchester Middle/High School, Eastchester, NY and Westchester Community College, NY

Alfred J. Valentini, T. R. Proctor High School, Utica, NY

Standards for Japanese Language Learning (2012)

A collaborative project of the National Council of Japanese Language Teachers and the Association of Teachers of Japanese (Now: The American Association of Teachers of Japanese)

Japanese National Standards Task Force

Pamela Delfosse, Madison West High School, Madison, WI

Yumiko Guajardo, U. S. Air Force Academy, Colorado Springs, CO

Kimberly Jones, University of Arizona, Tempe, AZ

Yoko Kano, University of North Carolina at Wilmington, Wilmington, NC

Hiroko Kataoka (Chair), California State University, Long Beach/Japan Foundation and Language Center, Santa Monica, CA

Waunita Kinoshita, Urbana High School, Urbana, IL

Norman Masuda, Palo Alto High School, Palo Alto, CA

Toyoko Okawa, Punahou School, Honolulu, HI

Carrie Penning, East Hartford Glastonbury Magnet School, East Hartford, CT

Jessica Thurrott, Maloney Magnet School, Waterbury, CT

Yasu-Hiko Tohsaku, University of California, San Diego, CA

Yasuko Ito Watt, Indiana University, Bloomington, IN

Standards for Korean Language Learning (2012)

A collaborative project of the Korean National Standards Task Force and the American Association of Teachers of Korean (AATK)

Korean National Standards Task Force

Sungdai Cho (Co-Chair), SUNY at Binghamton, Binghamton, NY

Young-mee Yu Cho (Co-Chair), Rutgers University, New Brunswick, NJ
Bruce Ballard, Charter School for Better Learning, Bronx, NY
Ah-mi Cho, Lowell High School, San Francisco, CA
Mikyong Cho, M.S. 142, Bronx, NY
Sunmi Choe, La Canada High School, La Canada, CA
Yongchul Chung, Sogang University, Seoul, Korea
Seonhwa Eun, Illinois State Board of Education, Springfield, IL
Sahie Kang, Defense Language Institute, Monterey, CA
Eunjung Kim, New Hope Academy, Landover Hills, MD
Hae-Young Kim, Duke University, Durham, NC
Hi-Sun Kim, University of Chicago, Chicago, IL
Dong Kwan Kong, University of Hawai'i at Mānoa, Honolulu, HI
Hyo Sang Lee, Indiana University, Bloomington, IN
Susan Strauss, Pennsylvania State University, University Park, PA
Joowon Suh, Princeton University, Princeton, NJ
Naehi Wong, Keppel Elementary School, Glendale, CA

Standards for Learning Portuguese (1999)

A project of the American Association of Teachers of Spanish and Portuguese

K–16 Task Force on Standards for Learning Portuguese

Nancy Anderson, Princeton, NJ
Rosario Cantú, Health Careers High School, San Antonio, TX
José M. Díaz, Hunter College High School, New York, NY
Inés García, Texas Education Agency, Austin, TX
Gail Guntermann, Arizona State University, Tempe, AZ
Nancy Humbach, Miami University, Oxford, OH
Judith Liskin-Gasparro, University of Iowa, Iowa City, IA
Donna R. Long, The Ohio State University, Columbus, OH
Frank Medley, Jr. (Team Leader), West Virginia University, Morgantown, WV
Myriam Met, Montgomery County Public Schools, Rockville, MD
Marilyn Pavlik (ex-officio), Lyons Township Schools, LaGrange, IL
Alvaro Rodríguez, MB Lamar High School and University of St. Thomas, Houston, TX
Paul Sandrock, Wisconsin Department of Public Instruction, Madison, WI
Lynn A. Sandstedt, American Association of Teachers of Spanish and Portuguese, Greeley, CO
Martie Semmer, Summit School District RE-1, Frisco, CO
Carmen C. Tesser (Chair), University of Georgia, Athens, GA
Guadalupe Valdés, Stanford University, Stanford, CA

Standards for Russian Language Learning (1999)

A Project of the American Council of Teachers of Russian/American Council for Collaboration in Education and Language Study

Authors

Ruth Edelman, Tenafly High School, NJ

Peter Merrill, Phillips Academy, Andover, MA
Jane Shuffelton, Brighton High School, Rochester, NY

Consultant
Thomas Garza, University of Texas, Austin

Reviewers
Thomas R. Beyer, Jr., Middlebury College, VT
Roald Sagdeev, University of Maryland, College Park
Thomas Welch, Jessamine High School, Nicholasville, KY
John Webb, Hunter College High School, New York, NY

Russian Representative, Board of Directors, Collaborative Project for National Standards in Foreign Language Learning
Dan E. Davidson, ACTR, Washington, DC and Bryn Mawr College, PA

Standards for Learning Scandinavian Languages (2012)

The Task Force for Standards for Learning Scandinavian Languages
Allison J. Spenader (Chair), Dean of *Sjölunden* Swedish Language Village, Concordia
    Language Villages, Moorhead, MN; College of St. Benedict and St. John's University, St.
    Joseph, MN
Ann-Marie Andreasson-Hogg, North Park University, Chicago, IL
Susan C. Brantly, University of Wisconsin, Madison, WI
Ia Dubois, University of Washington, Seattle, WA
Louis Janus, Center for Advanced Research on Language Acquisition, University of
    Minnesota, Minneapolis, MN
Gergana May, Indiana University, Bloomington, IN
Scott A. Mellor, University of Wisconsin, Madison, WI
Karen Møller, University of California, Berkeley, CA
Margaret Hayford O'Leary, St. Olaf College, Northfield, MN
Agnete Schmidt, University of Wisconsin, Madison, WI
Tanya Thresher, University of Wisconsin, Madison, WI
Charles Webster, University of Wisconsin, Madison, WI

Standards for Learning Spanish (1999)

A project of the American Association of Teachers of Spanish and Portuguese

K–16 Task Force on Standards for Learning Spanish
Nancy Anderson, Princeton, NJ
Rosario Cantú, Health Careers High School, San Antonio, TX
José M. Díaz, Hunter College High School, New York, NY
Inés García, Texas Education Agency, Austin, TX
Gail Guntermann (Chair), Arizona State University, Tempe, AZ
Nancy Humbach, Miami University, Oxford, OH
Judith Liskin-Gasparro, University of Iowa, Iowa City, IA
Donna R. Long (Team Leader), The Ohio State University, Columbus, OH

Frank Medley, Jr. (Team Leader), West Virginia University, Morgantown, WV

Myriam Met, Montgomery County Public Schools, Rockville, MD

Marilyn Pavlik (ex-officio), Lyons Township Schools, LaGrange, IL

Alvaro Rodríguez, MB Lamar High School and University of St. Thomas, Houston, TX

Paul Sandrock, Wisconsin Department of Public Instruction, Madison, WI

Lynn A. Sandstedt, American Association of Teachers of Spanish and Portuguese, Greeley, CO

Martie Semmer, Summit School District RE-1, Frisco, CO

Carmen C. Tesser (Team Leader), University of Georgia, Athens, GA

Guadalupe Valdés, Stanford University, Stanford, CA